# Practical LXC and LXD

## Linux Containers for Virtualization and Orchestration

Senthil Kumaran S.

Apress®

***Practical LXC and LXD***

Senthil Kumaran S.
Chennai, Tamil Nadu, India

ISBN-13 (pbk): 978-1-4842-3023-7          ISBN-13 (electronic): 978-1-4842-3024-4
DOI 10.1007/978-1-4842-3024-4

Library of Congress Control Number: 2017953000

Cover image designed by Freepik

Managing Director: Welmoed Spahr
Editorial Director: Todd Green
Acquisitions Editor: Nikhil Karkal
Development Editor: Matthew Moodie
Technical Reviewer: Steve McIntyre
Coordinating Editor: Prachi Mehta
Copy Editor: Bill McManus
Compositor: SPi Global
Indexer: SPi Global
Artist: SPi Global

Distributed to the book trade worldwide by Springer Science+Business Media New York, 233 Spring Street, 6th Floor, New York, NY 10013. Phone 1-800-SPRINGER, fax (201) 348-4505, e-mail orders-ny@springer-sbm.com, or visit www.springeronline.com. Apress Media, LLC is a California LLC and the sole member (owner) is Springer Science + Business Media Finance Inc (SSBM Finance Inc). SSBM Finance Inc is a **Delaware** corporation.

For information on translations, please e-mail rights@apress.com, or visit http://www.apress.com/rights-permissions.

Apress titles may be purchased in bulk for academic, corporate, or promotional use. eBook versions and licenses are also available for most titles. For more information, reference our Print and eBook Bulk Sales web page at http://www.apress.com/bulk-sales.

Any source code or other supplementary material referenced by the author in this book is available to readers on GitHub via the book's product page, located at www.apress.com/978-1-4842-3023-7. For more detailed information, please visit http://www.apress.com/source-code.

Printed on acid-free paper

*To my Father, who taught me "B.B. Roy of Great Britain Has a Very Good Wife."*

# Contents at a Glance

# Contents

# About the Author

**Senthil Kumaran S.,** popularly called "stylesen" on the Internet, is from Chennai, India, and is currently working as a LAVA Software Engineer for Linaro Ltd., in Cambridge, UK. He is a free software enthusiast and contributes to many free open source software projects. He is a Full Committer of the Apache Subversion version control system project and a Project Management Committee (PMC) member at Apache Software Foundation. As a Debian Maintainer, Senthil maintains packages such as django-compat and many Linaro Automated Validation Architecture (LAVA)-related packages for the Debian operating system. He has previously authored the book *Open Source* in the Tamil language. Senthil has contributed many articles to *Linux For You* magazine and is a regular speaker at various technical events. He holds a bachelor's degree in Computer Science and Engineering from Thiagarajar College of Engineering, Madurai, India, and a master's degree in Software Systems from Birla Institute of Technology, Pilani, India.

# About the Technical Reviewer

**Steve McIntyre** is a long-time contributor to a range of different Open Source projects but is best known as a developer and Project Leader Emeritus in the Debian project. He lives in Cambridge, England with his wife and their dog.

# Acknowledgments

I have been associated with the Linaro Automated Validation Architecture (LAVA) project for the past 5 years, which is almost from the beginning days of the project. Introduction of Linux Containers (LXC) in the LAVA project has solved many hard to address or complex use cases. This experience I gained with LXC in LAVA is the primary cause for writing this book.

I would like to thank Neil Williams, who leads the LAVA project at Linaro Ltd., for giving me the go-ahead when I floated the idea of writing this book. Steve McIntyre instantaneously accepted the invitation to be the technical reviewer of this book, and he has offered many non-trivial technical suggestions with extraordinary care and commitment to bring this book into the shape it is today. I would like to thank Stephane Graber for his excellent documentation on this topic, from which I started learning about LXC and LXD.

I thank Nikhil Karkal, Apress Acquisitions Editor, who gave me an opportunity and complete freedom right from choosing the idea/topic of this book. Matthew Moodie and Prachi Mehta from Apress helped me to plan and organize the chapters, and were instrumental in realizing this book as planned.

I would like to thank my family and friends, who were the primary source of encouragement to pursue things in my life. Special thanks to my wife, who comes from a medical background but still listened to my endless rants (typically late night) about Linux Containers and my narration of each word before it entered this book.

# CHAPTER 1

■ ■ ■

# Introduction to Linux Containers

Computer science is a field that keeps evolving at a very fast pace, requiring everyone in this industry to keep up to date on the latest technological advancements. In recent history, this industry has welcomed new technologies such as distributed computing, parallel processing, virtualization, cloud computing, and, most recently, the Internet of Things (IoT). Each technology paves the way for the next and helps to build a strong foundation for others. For example, virtualization revolutionized and built the basis for cloud computing. It has been common practice to use computers with maximum resource utilization from the beginning when computers were invented, whether via time sharing, multitasking, or the recent virtualization trends.

Since the early 1990s when the Linux kernel came into existence, many operating system distributions have evolved around the Linux kernel. However, until recently, GNU/Linux was used extensively only by advanced users with the skills to configure and maintain it. That has changed with the introduction of user-friendly interfaces by several GNU/Linux vendors, and now GNU/Linux is more widely adopted by consumer users on desktops, laptops, and so forth. With the advent of Linux kernel–powered Android phones, use of Linux has become ubiquitous among a much larger audience.

Containerization is the next logical step in virtualization, and there is a huge buzz around this technology. Containers can provide virtualization at both the operating system level and the application level. This book focuses on the use of containerization technology with the Linux kernel.

Some of the possibilities with containers are as follows:

- Provide a complete operating system environment that is sandboxed (isolated)

- Allow packaging and isolation of applications with their entire runtime environment

- Provide a portable and lightweight environment

- Help to maximize resource utilization in data centers

- Aid different development, test, and production deployment workflows

© Senthil Kumaran S. 2017
S. Kumaran S., *Practical LXC and LXD*, DOI 10.1007/978-1-4842-3024-4_1

# Container Definition

A container can be defined as a single operating system image, bundling a set of isolated applications and their dependent resources so that they run separated from the host machine. There may be multiple such containers running within the same host machine.

Containers can be classified into two types:

- *Operating system level*: An entire operating system runs in an isolated space within the host machine, sharing the same kernel as the host machine.

- *Application level*: An application or service, and the minimal processes required by that application, runs in an isolated space within the host machine.

Containerization differs from traditional virtualization technologies and offers many advantages over traditional virtualization:

- Containers are lightweight compared to traditional virtual machines.

- Unlike containers, virtual machines require emulation layers (either software or hardware), which consume more resources and add additional overhead.

- Containers share resources with the underlying host machine, with user space and process isolations.

- Due to the lightweight nature of containers, more containers can be run per host than virtual machines per host.

- Starting a container happens nearly instantly compared to the slower boot process of virtual machines.

- Containers are portable and can reliably regenerate a system environment with required software packages, irrespective of the underlying host operating system.

Figure 1-1 illustrates the differences in how virtual machines, Linux Containers (LXC) or operating system–level containers, and application-level containers are organized within a host operating system.

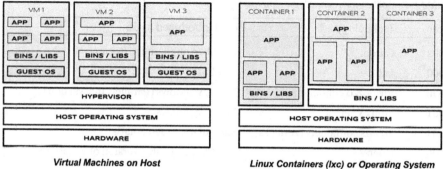

Virtual Machines on Host    Linux Containers (lxc) or Operating System Level Containers

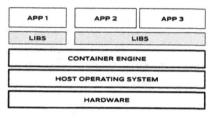

Application Level Containers

*Figure 1-1.* *Comparing virtual machines, LXC or OS-level containers, and application-level containers*

# Container History

Virtualization was developed as an effort to fully utilize available computing resources. Virtualization enables multiple virtual machines to run on a single host for different purposes with their own isolated space. Virtualization achieved such isolated operating system environments using *hypervisors*, computer software that sits in between the host operating system and the guest or the virtual machine's operating system. As mentioned in the introduction, containerization is the next logical step in virtualization, providing virtualization at both the operating system level and the application level.

Container technology has existed for a long time in different forms, but it has significantly gained popularity recently in the Linux world with the introduction of native containerization support in the Linux kernel. Table 1-1 lists some of the earlier related techniques that have led us to the current state of the art.

*Table 1-1.* *Container Technology Timeline*

| Year | Technology | First Introduced in OS |
|------|-----------|------------------------|
| 1982 | Chroot | Unix-like operating systems |
| 2000 | Jail | FreeBSD |
| 2000 | Virtuozzo containers | Linux, Windows (Parallels Inc. version) |
| 2001 | Linux VServer | Linux, Windows |
| 2004 | Solaris containers (zones) | Sun Solaris, Open Solaris |
| 2005 | OpenVZ | Linux (open source version of Virtuozzo) |
| 2008 | LXC | Linux |
| 2013 | Docker | Linux, FreeBSD, Windows |

■ **Note** Some technologies covered in Table 1-1 may be supported in more operating systems than those listed. Most of the technologies are available on various forms of Unix operating system, including Linux.

Some container technologies listed in Table 1-1 have a very specific purpose, such as chroot, which provides filesystem isolation by switching the root directory for running processes and their children. Other technologies listed provide complete operating system–level virtualization, such as Solaris containers (zones) and LXC.

Common modern-day containers are descended from LXC, which was first introduced in 2008. LXC was possible due to some key features added to the Linux kernel starting from the 2.6.24 release, as described in the next section.

# Features to Enable Containers

Containers rely on the following features in the Linux kernel to get a contained or isolated area within the host machine. This area is closely related to a virtual machine, but without the need for a hypervisor.

- Control groups (cgroups)
- Namespaces
- Filesystem or rootfs

## Control Groups (Cgroups)

To understand the importance of cgroups, consider a common scenario: A process running on a system requests certain resources from the system at a particular instance, but unfortunately the resources are unavailable currently, so the system decides to defer the process until the requested resources are available. The requested resources may become available when other processes release them. This delays the process execution, which may not be acceptable in many applications. Resource unavailability such as this can occur when a malicious process consumes all or a majority of the resources available on a system and does not allow other processes to execute.

Google presented a new generic method to solve the resource control problem with the cgroups project in 2007. Control groups allow resources to be controlled and accounted for based on process groups. The mainline Linux kernel first included a cgroups implementation in 2008, and this paved the way for LXC.

Cgroups provide a mechanism to aggregate sets of tasks or processes and their future children into hierarchical groups. These groups may be configured to have specialized behavior as desired.

## Listing Cgroups

Cgroups are listed within the pseudo filesystem subsystem in the directory /sys/fs/cgroup, which gives an overview of all the cgroup subsystems available or mounted in the currently running system:

```
stylesen@harshu:~$ ls -alh /sys/fs/cgroup
total 0
drwxr-xr-x 12 root root 320 Mar 24 20:40 .
drwxr-xr-x  8 root root   0 Mar 24 20:40 ..
dr-xr-xr-x  6 root root   0 Mar 24 20:40 blkio
lrwxrwxrwx  1 root root  11 Mar 24 20:40 cpu -> cpu,cpuacct
lrwxrwxrwx  1 root root  11 Mar 24 20:40 cpuacct -> cpu,cpuacct
dr-xr-xr-x  6 root root   0 Mar 24 20:40 cpu,cpuacct
dr-xr-xr-x  3 root root   0 Mar 24 20:40 cpuset
dr-xr-xr-x  6 root root   0 Mar 24 20:40 devices
dr-xr-xr-x  4 root root   0 Mar 24 20:40 freezer
dr-xr-xr-x  7 root root   0 Mar 24 20:40 memory
lrwxrwxrwx  1 root root  16 Mar 24 20:40 net_cls -> net_cls,net_prio
dr-xr-xr-x  3 root root   0 Mar 24 20:40 net_cls,net_prio
lrwxrwxrwx  1 root root  16 Mar 24 20:40 net_prio -> net_cls,net_prio
dr-xr-xr-x  3 root root   0 Mar 24 20:40 perf_event
dr-xr-xr-x  6 root root   0 Mar 24 20:40 pids
dr-xr-xr-x  7 root root   0 Mar 24 20:40 systemd
```

## Memory Subsystem Hierarchy

Let's take a look at an example of the memory subsystem hierarchy of cgroups. It is available in the following location:

```
/sys/fs/cgroup/memory
```

The memory subsystem hierarchy consists of the following files:

```
root@harshu:/sys/fs/cgroup/memory# ls
cgroup.clone_children              memory.memsw.failcnt
cgroup.event_control               memory.memsw.limit_in_bytes
cgroup.procs                       memory.memsw.max_usage_in_bytes
cgroup.sane_behavior               memory.memsw.usage_in_bytes
init.scope                         memory.move_charge_at_immigrate
lxc                                memory.numa_stat
memory.failcnt                     memory.oom_control
memory.force_empty                 memory.pressure_level
memory.kmem.failcnt                memory.soft_limit_in_bytes
memory.kmem.limit_in_bytes         memory.stat
memory.kmem.max_usage_in_bytes     memory.swappiness
memory.kmem.slabinfo               memory.usage_in_bytes
memory.kmem.tcp.failcnt            memory.use_hierarchy
memory.kmem.tcp.limit_in_bytes     notify_on_release
memory.kmem.tcp.max_usage_in_bytes release_agent
memory.kmem.tcp.usage_in_bytes     system.slice
memory.kmem.usage_in_bytes         tasks
memory.limit_in_bytes              user
memory.max_usage_in_bytes          user.slice
root@harshu:/sys/fs/cgroup/memory#
```

Each of the files listed contains information on the control group for which it has been created. For example, the maximum memory usage in bytes is given by the following command (since this is the top-level hierarchy, it lists the default setting for the current host system):

```
root@harshu:/sys/fs/cgroup/memory# cat memory.max_usage_in_bytes
15973715968
```

The preceding value is in bytes; it corresponds to approximately 14.8GB of memory that is available for use by the currently running system. You can create your own cgroups within /sys/fs/cgroup and control each of the subsystems.

## Namespaces

At the Ottawa Linux Symposium held in 2006, Eric W. Bierderman presented his paper "Multiple Instances of the Global Linux Namespaces" (available at https://www.kernel.org/doc/ols/2006/ols2006v1-pages-101-112.pdf). This paper proposed the addition of ten namespaces to the Linux kernel. His inspiration for these additional namespaces was the existing filesystem namespace for mounts, which was introduced in 2002. The proposed namespaces are as follows:

- The Filesystem Mount Namespace (mnt)

- The UTS Namespace

- The IPC Namespace (ipc)

- The Network Namespace (net)

- The Process Id Namespace (pid)

- The User and Group ID Namespace

- Security Modules and Namespaces

- The Security Keys Namespace

- The Device Namespace

- The Time Namespace

A namespace provides an abstraction to a global system resource that will appear to the processes within the defined namespace as its own isolated instance of a specific global resource. Namespaces are used to implement containers; they provide the required isolation between a container and the host system.

Over time, different namespaces have been implemented in the Linux kernel. As of this writing, there are seven namespaces implemented in the Linux kernel, which are listed in Table 1-2.

*Table 1-2.* *Existing Linux Namespaces*

| Namespace | Constant | Isolates |
|-----------|----------|----------|
| Cgroup | CLONE_NEWCGROUP | Cgroup root directory |
| IPC | CLONE_NEWIPC | System V IPC, POSIX message queues |
| Network | CLONE_NEWNET | Network devices, stacks, ports, etc. |
| Mount | CLONE_NEWNS | Mount points |
| PID | CLONE_NEWPID | Process IDs |
| User | CLONE_NEWUSER | User and group IDs |
| UTS | CLONE_NEWUTS | Hostname and NIS domain name |

Let's examine how namespaces work with the help of a simple example using the network namespace.

# Simple Network Namespace

Namespaces are created by passing the appropriate clone flags to the clone() system call. There is a command-line interface for the network namespace that can be used to illustrate a simple network namespace, as follows:

---

■ **Note**   Root privileges are required to create a network namespace.

---

7

1.  Create a network namespace called `stylesen-net`:

    ```
    # ip netns add stylesen-net
    ```

2.  To list all devices present in the newly created network
    namespace, issue the following command. This example
    shows the default loopback device.

    ```
    # ip netns exec stylesen-net ip link list
    1: lo: <LOOPBACK> mtu 65536 qdisc noop state DOWN mode
    DEFAULT group default qlen 1
            link/loopback 00:00:00:00:00:00 brd 00:00:00:00:00:00
    ```

3.  Try to ping the loopback device:

    ```
    # ip netns exec stylesen-net ping 127.0.0.1
    connect: Network is unreachable
    ```

4.  Though the loopback device is available, it is not up yet. Bring
    up the loopback device and try pinging it again:

    ```
    # ip netns exec stylesen-net ip link set dev lo up
    # ip netns exec stylesen-net ping 127.0.0.1PING 127.0.0.1
    (127.0.0.1) 56(84) bytes of data.
    64 bytes from 127.0.0.1: icmp_seq=1 ttl=64 time=0.045 ms
    64 bytes from 127.0.0.1: icmp_seq=2 ttl=64 time=0.059 ms
    64 bytes from 127.0.0.1: icmp_seq=3 ttl=64 time=0.097 ms
    64 bytes from 127.0.0.1: icmp_seq=4 ttl=64 time=0.084 ms
    64 bytes from 127.0.0.1: icmp_seq=5 ttl=64 time=0.095 ms
    ^C
    --- 127.0.0.1 ping statistics ---
    5 packets transmitted, 5 received, 0% packet loss, time 4082ms
    rtt min/avg/max/mdev = 0.045/0.076/0.097/0.020 ms
    ```

Thus, we can create network namespaces and add devices to them. Any number of
network namespaces can be created, and then different network configurations can be
set up between the devices available in these individual namespaces.

## Filesystem or rootfs

The next component needed for a container is the disk image, which provides the root
filesystem (rootfs) for the container. The rootfs consists of a set of files, similar in structure
to the filesystem mounted at root on any GNU/Linux-based machine. The size of rootfs is
smaller than a typical OS disk image, since it does not contain the kernel. The container
shares the same kernel as the host machine.

A rootfs can further be reduced in size by making it contain just the application and configuring it to share the rootfs of the host machine. Using copy-on-write (COW) techniques, a single reduced read-only disk image may be shared between multiple containers.

# Summary

This chapter introduced you to the world of container technology with a comparison of containers to traditional virtualization technologies that use virtual machines. You also saw a brief history of container technology and the important Linux kernel features that were introduced to underpin modern container technologies. The chapter wrapped up with an overview of the three basic features (cgroups, namespaces, and rootfs) that enable containerization.

# CHAPTER 2

■ ■ ■

# Installation

This chapter explains the installation steps for LXC and LXD in Ubuntu GNU/Linux. If you have already installed LXC and LXD and have a working setup, then you can safely skip this chapter.

LXC is supported by all modern GNU/Linux distributions, and there should already be an LXC package available from the standard package repositories for your distro.

The installation, illustrations, and examples throughout this book demonstrate version 2.0.7 of the LXC userspace tools and version 2.12 of LXD. These are the default versions available in the Ubuntu Zesty Zapus (17.04) release, as of this writing. The host operating system used here is Ubuntu Zesty Zapus (17.04) unless otherwise specified.

## LXC Installation

LXC installation involves the installation of userspace tools to deploy containers using the underlying kernel features. The following components are installed in a typical LXC installation:

- Set of userspace tools
- Templates
- Libraries
- Language bindings

There are two versions of the LXC userspace tools currently supported by upstream:

- LXC 1.0 (supported until June 1, 2019)
- LXC 2.0 (supported until June 1, 2021)

© Senthil Kumaran S. 2017
S. Kumaran S., *Practical LXC and LXD*, DOI 10.1007/978-1-4842-3024-4_2

# Installing LXC on Ubuntu

As in any Ubuntu-based system that is rich with packages from a default package repository, the installation of LXC involves the following command to install LXC userspace tools:

---

■ **Note** Ubuntu is a Debian-based distro. The same installation method applies for any Debian-based GNU/Linux distro. In case of a non-Debian-based distro, look for the method of installing LXC through its respective package manager.

---

```
$ sudo apt install lxc
Reading package lists... Done
Building dependency tree
Reading state information... Done
The following additional packages will be installed:
 bridge-utils cloud-image-utils debootstrap distro-info dns-root-data
 dnsmasq-base libaio1 libboost-random1.62.0 libiscsi7 liblxc1 libpam-cgfs
 librados2 librbd1 lxc-common lxc-templates lxc1 lxcfs python3-lxc
 qemu-block-extra qemu-utils sharutils uidmap
Suggested packages:
 cloud-utils-euca shunit2 qemu-user-static btrfs-tools lvm2 lxctl
 sharutils-doc bsd-mailx | mailx
The following NEW packages will be installed:
 bridge-utils cloud-image-utils debootstrap distro-info dns-root-data
 dnsmasq-base libaio1 libboost-random1.62.0 libiscsi7 liblxc1 libpam-cgfs
 librados2 librbd1 lxc lxc-common lxc-templates lxc1 lxcfs python3-lxc
 qemu-block-extra qemu-utils sharutils uidmap
0 upgraded, 23 newly installed, 0 to remove and 0 not upgraded.
Need to get 6,255 kB of archives.
After this operation, 25.6 MB of additional disk space will be used.
Do you want to continue? [Y/n] y
Get:1 http://in.archive.ubuntu.com/ubuntu zesty/main amd64 bridge-utils
amd64 1.5-9ubuntu2 [29.2 kB]
----------OUTPUT TRUNCATED----------
Setting up librbd1 (10.2.7-0ubuntu0.17.04.1) ...
Setting up qemu-block-extra:amd64 (1:2.8+dfsg-3ubuntu2.2) ...
Setting up qemu-utils (1:2.8+dfsg-3ubuntu2.2) ...
Setting up cloud-image-utils (0.30-0ubuntu2) ...
Setting up liblxc1 (2.0.7-0ubuntu2) ...
Setting up python3-lxc (2.0.7-0ubuntu2) ...
Setting up lxc-common (2.0.7-0ubuntu2) ...
Setting up lxc1 (2.0.7-0ubuntu2) ...
Created symlink /etc/systemd/system/multi-user.target.wants/lxc-net.service →
/lib/systemd/system/lxc-net.service.
```

```
Created symlink /etc/systemd/system/multi-user.target.wants/lxc.service →
/lib/systemd/system/lxc.service.
Setting up lxc dnsmasq configuration.
Setting up lxc (2.0.7-0ubuntu2) ...
Setting up lxc-templates (2.0.7-0ubuntu2) ...
Processing triggers for libc-bin (2.24-9ubuntu2) ...
Processing triggers for systemd (232-21ubuntu3) ...
Processing triggers for ureadahead (0.100.0-19) ...
$
```

■ **Note**    It is recommended to apt update and apt upgrade the Ubuntu Zesty host system before installing LXC packages to get the latest version of packages that LXC depends on directly or indirectly.

After installing LXC as just shown, the following commands will be available in the host system:

| | | |
|---|---|---|
| lxc-attach | lxc-create | lxc-snapshot |
| lxc-autostart | lxc-destroy | lxc-start |
| lxc-cgroup | lxc-device | lxc-start-ephemeral |
| lxc-checkconfig | lxc-execute | lxc-stop |
| lxc-checkpoint | lxc-freeze | lxc-top |
| lxc-clone | lxcfs | lxc-unfreeze |
| lxc-config | lxc-info | lxc-unshare |
| lxc-console | lxc-ls | lxc-usernsexec |
| lxc-copy | lxc-monitor | lxc-wait |

Each of the preceding commands has its own dedicated manual (man) page, which provides a handy reference for the usage of, available options for, and additional information about the command.

For LXC userspace tools to work properly in the host operating system, you must ensure that all the kernel features required for LXC support are enabled in the running host kernel. This can be verified using lxc-checkconfig, provided by the LXC package that you just installed. Everything listed in the lxc-checkconfig command output should have the status enabled; otherwise, try restarting the system. Sample output of the lxc-checkconfig command is as follows:

```
$ lxc-checkconfig
Kernel configuration not found at /proc/config.gz; searching...
Kernel configuration found at /boot/config-4.10.0-22-generic
--- Namespaces ---
Namespaces: enabled
Utsname namespace: enabled
Ipc namespace: enabled
```

```
Pid namespace: enabled
User namespace: enabled
Network namespace: enabled

--- Control groups ---
Cgroup: enabled
Cgroup clone_children flag: enabled
Cgroup device: enabled
Cgroup sched: enabled
Cgroup cpu account: enabled
Cgroup memory controller: enabled
Cgroup cpuset: enabled

--- Misc ---
Veth pair device: enabled
Macvlan: enabled
Vlan: enabled
Bridges: enabled
Advanced netfilter: enabled
CONFIG_NF_NAT_IPV4: enabled
CONFIG_NF_NAT_IPV6: enabled
CONFIG_IP_NF_TARGET_MASQUERADE: enabled
CONFIG_IP6_NF_TARGET_MASQUERADE: enabled
CONFIG_NETFILTER_XT_TARGET_CHECKSUM: enabled
FUSE (for use with lxcfs): enabled

--- Checkpoint/Restore ---
checkpoint restore: enabled
CONFIG_FHANDLE: enabled
CONFIG_EVENTFD: enabled
CONFIG_EPOLL: enabled
CONFIG_UNIX_DIAG: enabled
CONFIG_INET_DIAG: enabled
CONFIG_PACKET_DIAG: enabled
CONFIG_NETLINK_DIAG: enabled
File capabilities: enabled

Note : Before booting a new kernel, you can check its configuration
usage : CONFIG=/path/to/config /usr/bin/lxc-checkconfig

$
```

---

■ **Note**   The host system where the LXC package is installed in the preceding example runs the "Linux 4.10.0-22-generic #24-Ubuntu SMP Mon May 22 17:43:20 UTC 2017 x86_64 GNU/Linux" Linux kernel version available as the default from Ubuntu Zesty Zapus installation without any modifications to the Linux kernel or the host system.

---

## LXC Default Configuration

/etc/lxc/default.conf is the default configuration file for LXC installed using the standard Ubuntu packages. This configuration file supplies the default configuration for all containers created on the host system. Container-specific overrides can be configured in an individual container's configuration file, typically found in /var/lib/lxc/ {container-name}/config.

The default configuration file /etc/lxc/default.conf contains the following lines after installation:

```
$ cat /etc/lxc/default.conf
lxc.network.type = veth
lxc.network.link = lxcbr0
lxc.network.flags = up
lxc.network.hwaddr = 00:16:3e:xx:xx:xx
$
```

The networking will be set up as a virtual Ethernet connection type—that is, veth from the network bridge lxcbr0 for each container that will get created.

## Networking Setup for LXC

By default, a container runs an isolated operating system environment. If the operating system should communicate with systems outside the container, you will need to configure networking for it. Ubuntu Zesty's LXC package includes a default networking setup for LXC using a bridge.

If your operating system does not include a default networking setup, then the following sections will be useful. There is more than one way of setting up the network for LXC depending upon your networking needs. Let's look at a couple of easy methods to do this.

## Using a Bridge

The latest LXC package has some default networking scripts that get enabled to set up bridge networking for LXC containers. This could be configured by creating a configuration file /etc/default/lxc-net containing the following settings:

---

■ **Note**    Install bridge-utils (if it is not already installed) by using the following command. The bridge-utils package provides related tools to establish a bridge network.

```
$ sudo apt install bridge-utils
```

---

```
USE_LXC_BRIDGE="true"
LXC_BRIDGE="lxcbr0"
LXC_ADDR="10.0.0.1"
LXC_NETMASK="255.255.255.0"
LXC_NETWORK="10.0.0.0/24"
LXC_DHCP_RANGE="10.0.0.2,10.0.0.254"
LXC_DHCP_MAX="253"
LXC_DHCP_CONFILE=""
LXC_DOMAIN=""
```

With these settings, a default bridged network will be created for every container that is created in the host system with the help of the script /usr/lib/x86_64-linux-gnu /lxc/lxc-net.

---

■ **Note**    The file /etc/default/lxc-net is not available after installation of the LXC package and it should be created by the user.

---

Alternatively, edit the file /etc/lxc/default.conf and replace the following content

```
lxc.network.type = empty
```

with

```
lxc.network.type = veth
lxc.network.link = lxcbr0
lxc.network.flags = up
lxc.network.hwaddr = 00:18:5e:xx:xx:xx
```

These settings will cause each newly created container to use networking based on the lxc-net service.

With either of the preceding configurations in place, start or restart the lxc-net service as follows:

```
$ sudo service lxc-net restart
```

This will ensure networking is available for each container that gets created on the host system.

## Using the libvirt Default Network

This method is recommended over setting up network using a bridge. Using a bridged network can get complicated at times, especially if you are testing using a laptop and you need to bridge the Wi-Fi network interface (if one is available). Bridging a Wi-Fi network interface is a tedious process and involves a lot of configuration, where libvirt can simplify network setup significantly, particularly in difficult situations like this.

Install the required packages and start the virtual bridge:

```
$ sudo apt install libvirt-clients libvirt-daemon-system ebtables dnsmasq
$ sudo virsh net-start default
$ /sbin/ifconfig -a
```

There should be a new virtual bridge seen as follows:

```
virbr0: flags=4099<UP,BROADCAST,MULTICAST>  mtu 1500
        inet 192.168.122.1  netmask 255.255.255.0  broadcast 192.168.122.255
        ether 52:54:00:ad:2c:7a  txqueuelen 1000  (Ethernet)
        RX packets 0  bytes 0 (0.0 B)
        RX errors 0  dropped 0  overruns 0  frame 0
        TX packets 0  bytes 0 (0.0 B)
        TX errors 0  dropped 0 overruns 0  carrier 0  collisions 0
```

Link all your containers to the new virtual bridge by editing /etc/lxc/default.conf to read:

```
$ sudo cat /etc/lxc/default.conf
lxc.network.type = veth
lxc.network.flags = up
lxc.network.link = virbr0
```

Next, make the default virtual network bridge interface automatically start when the host boots:

```
$ sudo virsh net-autostart default
$ sudo virsh net-info default
Name:           default
UUID:           xxxxxxxx-xxxx-xxxx-xxxx-xxxxxxxxxxxx
```

```
Active:         yes
Persistent:     yes
Autostart:      yes
Bridge:         virbr0
```

## Other Resources

The following other useful resources may help you set up networking for LXC in Debian-based operating systems:

- Network setup: https://wiki.debian.org/LXC#network_setup

- Simple bridge: https://wiki.debian.org/LXC/SimpleBridge

- Masqueraded bridge: https://wiki.debian.org/LXC/MasqueradedBridge

- VLAN networking: https://wiki.debian.org/LXC/VlanNetworking

# LXD Installation

LXD provides a new and better user experience to LXC by building on top of LXC. LXD uses liblxc and its Go language bindings to create and manage containers.

LXD is made of three components:

- A system-wide daemon (lxd)

- A command-line client (lxc)

- An OpenStack Nova plugin (nova-compute-lxd)

LXD is supported very well in Ubuntu-based distributions, but it is not packaged for Debian yet. The latest available version of the LXD package in Ubuntu Zesty Zapus (17.04) is 2.12.

## LXC Requirements for LXD

LXD 2.x requires LXC 2.0.0 or higher with the following build options:

- apparmor (if using LXD's apparmor support)

- seccomp

To run the recent version of various distributions, including Ubuntu, LXCFS should also be installed.

# Installing LXD on Ubuntu

On a Ubuntu system with a large repository of packages, the installation of LXD involves the following command. This installation uses an Ubuntu Zesty Zapus (17.04) host; the latest available version of LXD there is 2.12.

```
$ sudo apt install lxd
Reading package lists... Done
Building dependency tree
Reading state information... Done
The following additional packages will be installed:
 ebtables libgolang-1.7-std1 libgolang-github-gorilla-context1
 libgolang-github-gorilla-mux1 libgolang-github-gorilla-websocket1
 libgolang-github-gosexy-gettext1 libgolang-github-mattn-go-colorable1
 libgolang-github-mattn-go-sqlite3-1 libgolang-github-olekukonko-tablewriter1
 libgolang-github-pborman-uuid1 libgolang-gocapability1
 libgolang-golang-x-crypto1 libgolang-golang-x-net1 libgolang-golang-x-text1
 libgolang-gopkg-flosch-pongo2.v3-1
 libgolang-gopkg-inconshreveable-log15.v2-1 libgolang-gopkg-lxc-go-lxc.v2-1
 libgolang-gopkg-tomb.v2-1 libgolang-gopkg-yaml.v2-1 libgolang-goprotobuf1
 libgolang-petname1 lxd-client
Suggested packages:
 criu lxd-tools
The following NEW packages will be installed:
 ebtables libgolang-1.7-std1 libgolang-github-gorilla-context1
 libgolang-github-gorilla-mux1 libgolang-github-gorilla-websocket1
 libgolang-github-gosexy-gettext1 libgolang-github-mattn-go-colorable1
 libgolang-github-mattn-go-sqlite3-1 libgolang-github-olekukonko-tablewriter1
 libgolang-github-pborman-uuid1 libgolang-gocapability1
 libgolang-golang-x-crypto1 libgolang-golang-x-net1 libgolang-golang-x-text1
 libgolang-gopkg-flosch-pongo2.v3-1
 libgolang-gopkg-inconshreveable-log15.v2-1 libgolang-gopkg-lxc-go-lxc.v2-1
 libgolang-gopkg-tomb.v2-1 libgolang-gopkg-yaml.v2-1 libgolang-goprotobuf1
 libgolang-petname1 lxd lxd-client
0 upgraded, 23 newly installed, 0 to remove and 0 not upgraded.
Need to get 11.7 MB of archives.
After this operation, 56.6 MB of additional disk space will be used.
Do you want to continue? [Y/n] y
Get:1 http://in.archive.ubuntu.com/ubuntu zesty/main amd64 ebtables amd64
2.0.10.4-3.5ubuntu1 [80.1 kB]
----------OUTPUT TRUNCATED----------
Unpacking libgolang-goprotobuf1 (0.0~git20161116.0.224aaba-3ubuntu1) ...
Selecting previously unselected package lxd.
Preparing to unpack .../22-lxd_2.12-0ubuntu3_amd64.deb ...
Adding system user `lxd' (UID 126) ...
Adding new user `lxd' (UID 126) with group `nogroup' ...
```

```
Creating home directory `/var/lib/lxd/' ...
Adding group `lxd' (GID 133) ...
Done.
Unpacking lxd (2.12-0ubuntu3) ...
Processing triggers for ureadahead (0.100.0-19) ...
Setting up libgolang-1.7-std1 (1.7.4-2ubuntu1) ...
Setting up libgolang-gopkg-flosch-pongo2.v3-1 (3.0+git20141028.0.5e81b81-
0ubuntu7) ...
Setting up libgolang-github-mattn-go-sqlite3-1 (1.1.0~dfsg1-2ubuntu4) ...
Processing triggers for libc-bin (2.24-9ubuntu2) ...
Setting up libgolang-gopkg-lxc-go-lxc.v2-1 (0.0~git20161126.1.82a07a6-
0ubuntu3) ...
Processing triggers for systemd (232-21ubuntu3) ...
Setting up ebtables (2.0.10.4-3.5ubuntu1) ...
Created symlink /etc/systemd/system/multi-user.target.wants/ebtables.service →
/lib/systemd/system/ebtables.service.
----------OUTPUT TRUNCATED----------
Setting up lxd (2.12-0ubuntu3) ...
Created symlink /etc/systemd/system/multi-user.target.wants/ →
lxd-containers.service/lib/systemd/system/lxd-containers.service.
Created symlink /etc/systemd/system/sockets.target.wants/lxd.socket →
/lib/systemd/system/lxd.socket.
Setting up lxd dnsmasq configuration.

To go through the initial LXD configuration, run: lxd init

Processing triggers for libc-bin (2.24-9ubuntu2) ...
Processing triggers for systemd (232-21ubuntu3) ...
Processing triggers for ureadahead (0.100.0-19) ...
$
```

---

▓ **Note**    It is recommended to apt update and apt upgrade the Ubuntu host system
before installing LXD packages in order to get the latest version of packages that LXD
depends on directly or indirectly.

---

A new lxd group is created by the package, to control access to the lxd service. All
the users in the admin and sudoers groups on your host system will be automatically
added to this group, for convenience. If you need to grant lxd access to any other users,
add them to the lxd group too.

To continue interaction with lxd from your current shell session, use the following
command:

```
$ groups
stylesen adm cdrom sudo dip plugdev lpadmin sambashare
$ newgrp lxd
```

```
$ groups
lxd adm cdrom sudo dip plugdev lpadmin sambashare stylesen
$
```

Otherwise, you must close the current shell session and start a new one that has the correct group membership applied as it starts.

As the package installation stated, run the lxd init command to go through initial configuration of LXD. If you are satisfied with the default values, just press Enter to accept them and start the lxd service. The following output is a sample initial configuration run for lxd:

```
$ sudo lxd init
Do you want to configure a new storage pool (yes/no) [default=yes]?
Name of the new storage pool [default=default]:
Name of the storage backend to use (dir) [default=dir]:
Would you like LXD to be available over the network (yes/no) [default=no]? yes
Address to bind LXD to (not including port) [default=all]:
Port to bind LXD to [default=8443]:
Trust password for new clients:
Again:
Would you like stale cached images to be updated automatically (yes/no)
[default=yes]?
Would you like to create a new network bridge (yes/no) [default=yes]?
What should the new bridge be called [default=lxdbr0]?
What IPv4 address should be used (CIDR subnet notation, "auto" or "none")
[default=auto]?
What IPv6 address should be used (CIDR subnet notation, "auto" or "none")
[default=auto]?
LXD has been successfully configured.
$
```

Remember the trust password you previously supplied, which will be used by clients to contact this LXD server. If at a later time you have forgotten the trust password that you set during lxd init, you can run the following command from the LXD server to set a new password, where secret-password will be your new password:

```
$ sudo lxc config set core.trust_password secret-password
```

# Summary

It is very easy to install LXC and LXD in any Ubuntu- or Debian-based distribution using the package repositories of these distributions. It should be similarly easy to install and configure LXC and LXD in other common distributions too.

# CHAPTER 3

■ ■ ■

# Getting Started with LXC and LXD

At this point, you should have a working LXC and LXD installation in your host machine. This chapter steps you through the basic usage of LXC and LXD.

## Using LXC

LXC is a container within a host machine that runs a full-fledged operating system isolated from the host machine. LXC shares the same kernel as the host machine's kernel. In order to create different operating system containers we use templates which are scripts to bootstrap specific operating system.

## Templates

The templates provided in LXC are scripts specific to an operating system. Each operating system that is supported by the LXC installation has a script dedicated to it. There is also a generic script called "download" that can install many different operating systems with a common interface. As of this writing, the download template can install the operating system distributions described in Table 3-1.

© Senthil Kumaran S. 2017                                                                                      23
S. Kumaran S., *Practical LXC and LXD*, DOI 10.1007/978-1-4842-3024-4_3

***Table 3-1.*** *LXC 2.0.7 - Supported Distributions, Their Releases and Architectures*

| Distribution | Supported Releases | Supported Architectures |
|---|---|---|
| Alpine | 3.1, 3.2, 3.3, 3.4, 3.5, edge | amd64, armhf, i386 |
| ArchLinux | current | amd64, i386 |
| CentOS | 6, 7 | amd64, i386 |
| Debian | jessie, sid, stretch, wheezy | amd64, arm64, armel, armhf, i386, powerpc, ppc64el, s390x |
| Fedora | 22, 23, 24, 25 | amd64, i386 |
| Gentoo | current | amd64, i386 |
| openSUSE | 13.2, 42.2 | amd64 |
| Oracle | 6, 7 | amd64, i386 |
| Plamo | 5.x, 6.x | amd64, i386 |
| Ubuntu | precise, trusty, xenial, yakkety, zesty | amd64, arm64, armhf, i386, powerpc, ppc64el, s390x |

Note the following about Table 3-1:

- Debian Wheezy is not supported in arm64 and ppc64el architectures.

- Oracle 7 is not supported in i386 architecture.

- Ubuntu Precise is not supported in ppc64el and s390x. Ubuntu Trusty is not supported in s390x.

## Basic Usage

Figure 3-1 shows the life cycle of an LXC container with the various states the container can get into.

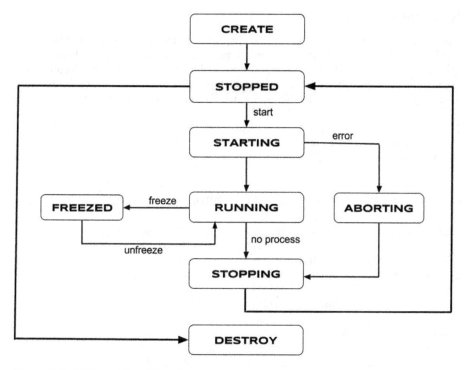

***Figure 3-1.*** *LXC container life cycle*

A simple LXC lifecycle will have the following steps:

1. lxc-create: Create a container with the given OS template and options.

2. lxc-start: Start running the container that was just created.

3. lxc-ls: List all the containers in the host system.

4. lxc-attach: Get a default shell session inside the container.

5. lxc-stop: Stop the running container, just like powering off a machine.

6. lxc-destroy: If the container will no longer be used, then destroy it.

## Using the Download Template

Let's look at how the preceding steps work in practice by creating a Debian Jessie container using the generic download template.

## lxc-create

The lxc-create command creates the container with the given OS template and options provided, if any. As shown next, the -t option specifies the template that should be used to create the container, which in our example is the download template. The -n option is mandatory for most of the LXC commands which specifies the name of the container or in other words the container identifier name, which is an alphanumeric string.

```
$ sudo lxc-create -t download -n example-debian-jessie
Setting up the GPG keyring
Downloading the image index

---
DIST        RELEASE    ARCH      VARIANT    BUILD
---
alpine      3.1        amd64     default    20170319_17:50
alpine      3.1        armhf     default    20161230_08:09
----------OUTPUT TRUNCATED----------
archlinux   current    amd64     default    20170505_01:27
archlinux   current    i386      default    20170504_01:27
centos      6          amd64     default    20170504_02:16
centos      6          i386      default    20170504_02:16
----------OUTPUT TRUNCATED----------
debian      stretch    amd64     default    20170504_02:41
debian      stretch    arm64     default    20170504_22:42
----------OUTPUT TRUNCATED----------
fedora      25         amd64     default    20170505_02:42
fedora      25         i386      default    20170504_01:27
gentoo      current    amd64     default    20170503_14:12
gentoo      current    i386      default    20170504_14:12
opensuse    13.2       amd64     default    20170320_00:53
opensuse    42.2       amd64     default    20170504_00:53
oracle      6          amd64     default    20170505_11:40
oracle      6          i386      default    20170505_12:47
----------OUTPUT TRUNCATED----------
plamo       6.x        amd64     default    20170504_22:05
plamo       6.x        i386      default    20170504_22:05
----------OUTPUT TRUNCATED----------
ubuntu      zesty      ppc64el   default    20170430_03:49
ubuntu      zesty      s390x     default    20170504_03:49
---

Distribution: debian
Release: jessie
Architecture: amd64

Downloading the image index
Downloading the rootfs
```

```
Downloading the metadata
The image cache is now ready
Unpacking the rootfs

---

You just created a Debian container (release=jessie, arch=amd64, variant=default)

To enable sshd, run: apt-get install openssh-server

For security reason, container images ship without user accounts
and without a root password.

Use lxc-attach or chroot directly into the rootfs to set a root password
or create user accounts.
$
```

Now you have created a Debian Jessie container called example-debian-jessie, using the amd64 architecture. As noted at the end of the lxc-create command, there are no user accounts nor root password set up in the container. You can use lxc-attach to start a shell session in the container later to make changes like this.

By default, the lxc-create command creates the containers in the directory /var/lib/lxc/{container-name}; for example, the new container will be created in the /var/lib/lxc/example-debian-jessie directory. The following shows the contents of the container directory:

```
$ sudo ls -alh /var/lib/lxc/example-debian-jessie
total 16K
drwxrwx--- 3 root root 4.0K Jun 12 14:47 .
drwx------ 4 root root 4.0K Jun 12 14:46 ..
-rw-r--r-- 1 root root  844 Jun 12 14:47 config
drwxr-xr-x 22 root root 4.0K May  4 08:55 rootfs
$ sudo ls /var/lib/lxc/example-debian-jessie/rootfs
bin   dev  home  lib64   mnt  proc  run   selinux  sys  usr
boot  etc  lib   media   opt  root  sbin  srv      tmp  var
$
```

The configuration specific to this container exists in /var/lib/lxc/example-debian-jessie/config, the contents of which are shown here:

```
$ sudo cat /var/lib/lxc/example-debian-jessie/config
# Template used to create this container: /usr/share/lxc/templates/lxc-download
# Parameters passed to the template: --release jessie --arch amd64
# Template script checksum (SHA-1): 740c51206e35463362b735e68b867876048a8baf
# For additional config options, please look at lxc.container.conf(5)

# Uncomment the following line to support nesting containers:
#lxc.include = /usr/share/lxc/config/nesting.conf
# (Be aware this has security implications)
```

```
# Distribution configuration
lxc.include = /usr/share/lxc/config/debian.common.conf
lxc.arch = x86_64

# Container specific configuration
lxc.rootfs = /var/lib/lxc/example-debian-jessie/rootfs
lxc.rootfs.backend = dir
lxc.utsname = example-debian-jessie

# Network configuration
lxc.network.type = veth
lxc.network.link = lxcbr0
lxc.network.flags = up
lxc.network.hwaddr = 00:16:3e:44:8e:e8
$
```

The default container creation path can be overridden using the -P option as shown here, which will create the container in /tmp directory:

```
$ sudo lxc-create -P /tmp/ -t download -n example-debian-jessie
```

---

■ **Note** Many lxc-* commands accept the -P option to access the container existing on a specific path. Refer to individual lxc-* command man pages to know which commands accept the -P option.

---

## lxc-start

Before we start using the container, we must first start it by using the lxc-start command. The -d option in lxc-start will start running the container in daemon mode, where the boot process output is not visible:

```
$ sudo lxc-start -d -n example-debian-jessie
```

Because -d is the default mode, it is not mandatory to specify it. To instead start running the container in foreground mode, we can use the -F option. This is useful to see debug messages and the entire boot process output. Here is sample output produced by starting our container in foreground mode:

```
$ sudo lxc-start -F -n example-debian-jessie
systemd 215 running in system mode. (+PAM +AUDIT +SELINUX +IMA +SYSVINIT
+LIBCRYPTSETUP +GCRYPT +ACL +XZ -SECCOMP -APPARMOR)
Detected virtualization 'lxc'.
Detected architecture 'x86-64'.

Welcome to Debian GNU/Linux 8 (jessie)!
```

Set hostname to <example-debian-jessie>.
Failed to install release agent, ignoring: No such file or directory
Cannot add dependency job for unit dbus.socket, ignoring: Unit dbus.socket
failed to load: No such file or directory.
[  OK  ] Reached target Remote File Systems (Pre).
[  OK  ] Reached target Paths.
[  OK  ] Reached target Encrypted Volumes.
----------OUTPUT TRUNCATED----------
         Starting Getty on tty4...
[  OK  ] Started Getty on tty4.
         Starting Getty on tty3...
[  OK  ] Started Getty on tty3.
         Starting Getty on tty2...
[  OK  ] Started Getty on tty2.
         Starting Getty on tty1...
[  OK  ] Started Getty on tty1.
         Starting Console Getty...
[  OK  ] Started Console Getty.
[  OK  ] Reached target Login Prompts.
[  OK  ] Reached target Multi-User System.
         Starting Update UTMP about System Runlevel Changes...
[  OK  ] Started Cleanup of Temporary Directories.
[  OK  ] Started Update UTMP about System Runlevel Changes.

Debian GNU/Linux 8 example-debian-jessie console

example-debian-jessie login:

## lxc-ls

This command lists the containers available in the host system:

```
$ sudo lxc-ls
example-debian-jessie
$
```

lxc-ls is also capable of showing more information with the --fancy option:

```
$ sudo lxc-ls --fancy
NAME                   STATE   AUTOSTART GROUPS IPV4       IPV6
example-debian-jessie RUNNING 0         -      10.0.3.206 -
$
```

lxc-ls comes in very handy to get an overview of all the containers in the host system.

## lxc-attach

Our container example-debian-jessie is now started and running. To log in or get access to a shell on the container, we can use lxc-attach as the first step. The lxc-attach command is used to start a process inside a running container; alternatively, if there are no commands supplied, then lxc-attach gives a shell session within the running container, as shown here:

```
$ sudo lxc-attach -n example-debian-jessie
root@example-debian-jessie:/# ls
bin   dev  home  lib64   mnt  proc  run    selinux  sys  usr
boot  etc  lib   media   opt  root  sbin   srv      tmp  var
root@example-debian-jessie:/# passwd
Enter new UNIX password:
Retype new UNIX password:
passwd: password updated successfully
root@example-debian-jessie:/# exit
$
```

---

■ **Note**   The preceding sample run shows how to reset the root password within the container.

---

## lxc-stop

Once we are done with our work with the container, we can stop the container. Stopping the container is equivalent to powering down a machine; we can start the container again any time in the future. Again, it is necessary to use the -n option to provide the name of the container when using lxc-stop:

```
$ sudo lxc-stop -n example-debian-jessie
```

After the container is stopped, the lxc-ls fancy output shows the status of the container as STOPPED, as follows, which also shows that the corresponding IPv4 address is released:

```
$ sudo lxc-ls --fancy
NAME                  STATE    AUTOSTART  GROUPS  IPV4  IPV6
example-debian-jessie STOPPED  0          -       -     -
$
```

## lxc-destroy

To permanently delete a container from the host system, use the lxc-destroy command. **This command is irreversible and any data or changes made within the container will be lost. Use this command only when you do not need the container any more.** Again, this command takes the name of the container that should be destroyed via the -n option:

```
$ sudo lxc-destroy -n example-debian-jessie
Destroyed container example-debian-jessie
$
```

# Using an OS Template

In this section, we will create a container using a specific OS template, following the same steps as in the previous section. You can find all the available LXC OS template scripts in /usr/share/lxc/templates. In an LXC 2.0.7 installation, the templates shown in Table 3-2 are available.

*Table 3-2.* OS Template Scripts in LXC 2.0.7

| | | |
|---|---|---|
| lxc-alpine | lxc-debian | lxc-plamo |
| lxc-altlinux | lxc-fedora | lxc-slackware |
| lxc-archlinux | lxc-gentoo | lxc-sparclinux |
| lxc-busybox | lxc-openmandriva | lxc-sshd |
| lxc-centos | lxc-opensuse | lxc-ubuntu |
| lxc-cirros | lxc-oracle | lxc-ubuntu-cloud |

In this case, let's use the fedora template as an example.

---

■ **Tip** To find the options available with any template, use the --help option on the template, which will provide the complete usage information about that particular template. For example:

```
$ sudo lxc-create -t fedora --help
```

---

## lxc-create

In case of OS-specific templates, it is good to specify the OS release explicitly, instead of making the OS-specific template script choose a default release. This is shown in the following lxc-create command execution, which creates a container with a fedora template named example-fedora-25 and specifies the Fedora release as 25:

31

```
$ sudo lxc-create -t fedora -n example-fedora-25 -- --release=25
Host CPE ID from /etc/os-release:
Checking cache download in /var/cache/lxc/fedora/x86_64/25/rootfs ...
Downloading fedora minimal ...
Fetching release rpm name from http://ftp.jaist.ac.jp/pub/Linux/Fedora/
releases/25/Everything/x86_64/os//Packages/f...
```

| % | Total | % | Received | % Xferd | Average Dload | Speed Upload | Time Total | Time Spent | Time Left | Current Speed |
|---|-------|---|----------|---------|--------------|-------------|-----------|-----------|----------|---------------|
| 100 | 392 | 100 | 392 | 0 0 | 820 | 0 | --:--:-- | --:--:-- | --:--:-- | 820 |
| 100 | 297k | 0 | 297k | 0 0 | 140k | 0 | --:--:-- | 0:00:02 | --:--:-- | 361k |

```
----------OUTPUT TRUNCATED----------
Bootstrap Environment testing...

Fedora Installation Bootstrap Build...

Downloading stage 0 LiveOS squashfs file system from archives.fedoraproject.org...
Have a beer or a cup of coffee. This will take a bit (~300MB).
----------OUTPUT TRUNCATED----------
receiving incremental file list
LiveOS/
LiveOS/squashfs.img
----------OUTPUT TRUNCATED----------
Container rootfs and config have been created.
Edit the config file to check/enable networking setup.
```

You have successfully built a Fedora container and cache. This cache may
be used to create future containers of various revisions. The directory
/var/cache/lxc/fedora/x86_64/bootstrap contains a bootstrap
which may no longer needed and can be removed.

A LiveOS directory exists at /var/cache/lxc/fedora/x86_64/LiveOS.
This is only used in the creation of the bootstrap run-time-environment
and may be removed.

The temporary root password is stored in:

        '/var/lib/lxc/example-fedora-25/tmp_root_pass'


The root password is set up as expired and will require it to be changed
at first login, which you should do as soon as possible. If you lose the
root password or wish to change it without starting the container, you
can change it from the host by running the following command (which will
also reset the expired flag):

        chroot /var/lib/lxc/example-fedora-25/rootfs passwd

$

---

■ **Note** The fedora template uses `curl` for downloading some artifacts, so you need to install `curl` using the following command if it is unavailable:

```
$ sudo apt install curl
```

---

As previously noted, the fedora template sets a temporary root password. Now we can proceed to start the container.

## lxc-start

The method of starting the container does not change with different templates:

```
$ sudo lxc-start -n example-fedora-25
```

## lxc-ls

Let's see the list of containers with their fancy status:

```
$ sudo lxc-ls --fancy
NAME                    STATE     AUTOSTART GROUPS IPV4          IPV6
example-fedora-25       RUNNING   0                10.0.3.207 -
$
```

## lxc-attach

Now let's run a shell session in our running container `example-fedora-25`:

```
$ sudo lxc-attach -n example-fedora-25
[root@example-fedora-25 /]# passwd
Changing password for user root.
New password:
Retype new password:
passwd: all authentication tokens updated successfully.
[root@example-fedora-25 /]# exit
$
```

## lxc-stop

The following command stops our running container `example-fedora-25`:

```
$ sudo lxc-stop -n example-fedora-25
$ sudo lxc-ls --fancy
NAME                    STATE     AUTOSTART GROUPS IPV4 IPV6
example-fedora-25       STOPPED 0           -       -    -
$
```

## lxc-destroy

To permanently delete our container example-fedora-25 from the host system, we use the lxc-destroy command as follows. Remember: **this command is irreversible and any data or changes made within the container will be lost. Use this command only when you do not need the container any more.**

```
$ sudo lxc-destroy -n example-fedora-25
Destroyed container example-fedora-25
$
```

# Using LXD

Unlike LXC, which uses an operating system template script to create its container, LXD uses an image as the basis for its container. It will download base images from a remote image store or make use of available images from a local image store. The image stores are simply LXD servers exposed over a network.

---

■ **Note** Somewhat confusingly, LXD also provides an lxc command. This is *different* from the lxc command in the LXC package described earlier. In the rest of this section, the lxc commands we use are for LXD. LXD uses liblxc APIs, hence the naming problems.

---

The image store that will be used by LXD can be populated using three methods:

- Using a remote LXD as an image server
- Using the built-in image remotes
- Manually importing an image

## Using a Remote LXD As an Image Server

A remote image server is added as a remote image store and you can start using it right away. The following output explains the same:

```
$ lxc remote add stylesen 192.168.1.8
$ lxc launch stylesen:image-name your-container
```

Here, 192.168.1.8 is the LXD image server that you have configured and is accessible from your host machine, and stylesen is the short name you provide for the remote LXD image server.

## Using the Built-in Remotes

By default, the LXD package configures three remotes and a local image store (local) that is communicated with via a local Unix socket. The three default remotes are as follows:

- images: For distros other than Ubuntu

- ubuntu: For stable Ubuntu images

- ubuntu-daily: For daily Ubuntu images

To get a list of remotes, use the following command:

```
$ lxc remote list
If this is your first time using LXD, you should also run: lxd init
To start your first container, try: lxc launch ubuntu:16.04
```

```
+----------------+------------------------------------+---------------+--------+--------+
|      NAME      |                URL                 |   PROTOCOL    | PUBLIC | STATIC |
+----------------+------------------------------------+---------------+--------+--------+
| images         | https://images.linuxcontainers.org | simplestreams | YES    | NO     |
+----------------+------------------------------------+---------------+--------+--------+
| local (default)| unix://                            |      lxd      | NO     | YES    |
+----------------+------------------------------------+---------------+--------+--------+
| ubuntu         | https://cloud-images.ubuntu.com/releases | simplestreams | YES | YES  |
+----------------+------------------------------------+---------------+--------+--------+
| ubuntu-daily   | https://cloud-images.ubuntu.com/daily | simplestreams | YES | YES   |
+----------------+------------------------------------+---------------+--------+--------+
$
```

## Manually Importing an Image

You can create LXD-compatible image files manually by following the specification available at https://github.com/lxc/lxd/blob/master/doc/image-handling.md. You can import the images that you create using this specification with the following command:

```
# lxc image import <file> --alias <my-alias>
```

# Running Your First Container with LXD

Before creating your first container, you should run lxd init as follows, if it has not run already:

```
$ lxd init
Do you want to configure a new storage pool (yes/no) [default=yes]?
Name of the new storage pool [default=default]:
Name of the storage backend to use (dir) [default=dir]:
Would you like LXD to be available over the network (yes/no) [default=no]? yes
```

```
Address to bind LXD to (not including port) [default=all]:
Port to bind LXD to [default=8443]:
Trust password for new clients:
Again:
Would you like stale cached images to be updated automatically (yes/no)
[default=yes]?
Would you like to create a new network bridge (yes/no) [default=yes]?
What should the new bridge be called [default=lxdbr0]?
What IPv4 address should be used (CIDR subnet notation, "auto" or "none")
[default=auto]?
What IPv6 address should be used (CIDR subnet notation, "auto" or "none")
[default=auto]?
LXD has been successfully configured.
$
```

You can import or copy an Ubuntu cloud image using the ubuntu: image store with the following command:

```
$ lxc image copy ubuntu:16.04 local: --alias ubuntu-xenial
Image copied successfully!
$
```

After importing the image to "local:": image-store, you can launch the first container with the following command:

```
$ lxc launch ubuntu-xenial first-lxd-container
Creating first-lxd-container
Starting first-lxd-container
$
```

The preceding command will create and start a new Ubuntu container named first-lxd-container, which can be confirmed with the following command:

```
$ lxc list
```

| NAME | STATE | IPV4 | IPV6 | TYPE | SNAPSHOTS |
|------|-------|------|------|------|-----------|
| first-lxd-container | RUNNING | 10.79. 218.118 (eth0) | fd42:fb6:bc78: 699c:216:3eff: fe54:28d (eth0) | PERSISTENT | 0 |

```
$
```

If the container name is not given, then LXD will give it a random name.

To get a shell inside a running container, use the following command:

```
$ lxc exec first-lxd-container -- /bin/bash
root@first-lxd-container:~# ls /
bin   dev  home  lib64  mnt  proc  run   snap  sys  usr
```

```
boot  etc  lib   media  opt  root  sbin  srv   tmp  var
root@first-lxd-container:~#
```

To run a command directly without starting a shell, use the following command:

```
$ lxc exec first-lxd-container -- apt-get update
```

Alternatively, you can use the lxc-console command provided by the lxc-tools package to connect to the LXD container:

```
$ sudo lxc-console -n first-lxd-container -P /var/lib/lxd/containers -t 0
```

```
Connected to tty 0
                Type <Ctrl+a q> to exit the console, <Ctrl+a Ctrl+a> to
                enter Ctrl+a itself

Ubuntu 16.04.2 LTS first-lxd-container console

first-lxd-container login:
$
```

The LXD containers are created by default in the /var/lib/lxd/containers/ directory. For example, the preceding LXD container (first-lxd-container) is created in /var/lib/lxd/containers/first-lxd-container, which in turn is a symbolic link (symlink) from the storage pool defined during lxc init. The lxc-console by default searches for the container in /var/lib/lxc/ since it is designed for LXC containers; hence, you need to pass the -P option to point to the LXD container default path. We can see how the LXD container creation default path is structured with the following:

```
$ sudo ls -alh /var/lib/lxd/containers/
total 16K
drwx--x--x   2 root root 4.0K Jun 12 14:21 .
drwxr-xr-x  12 lxd  nogroup 4.0K Jun 12 14:22 ..
lrwxrwxrwx   1 root root         65 Jun 12 14:21 first-lxd-container ->
/var/lib/lxd/storage-pools/default/containers/first-lxd-container
-rw-r--r--   1 root root 2.8K Jun 12 14:22 lxc-monitord.log
$ sudo ls -alh /var/lib/lxd/containers/first-lxd-container/
total 24K
drwxr-xr-x+  4 165536 165536 4.0K Jun 12 14:22 .
drwxr-xr-x   3 root   root   4.0K Jun 12 14:21 ..
-r--------   1 root   root   2.2K Jun 12 14:22 backup.yaml
-rw-r--r--   1 root   root   1.6K May 16 20:56 metadata.yaml
drwxr-xr-x v 22 165536 165536 4.0K May 16 19:49 rootfs
drwxr-xr-x   2 root   root   4.0K May 16 20:56 templates
$ sudo ls /var/lib/lxd/containers/first-lxd-container/rootfs/
bin   dev  home  lib64   mnt  proc  run    snap  sys  usr
boot  etc  lib   media   opt  root  sbin   srv   tmp  var
$
```

To copy a file from the container to your normal system, use the following command:

```
$ lxc file pull first-lxd-container/etc/hosts .
```

To put a file inside the container, use the following command:

```
$ lxc file push hosts first-lxd-container/tmp/
```

To stop a running container, use the following command, which will stop the container but keep the image so it may be restarted again later:

```
$ lxc stop first-lxd-container
$ lxc list
+---------------------+---------+------+------+------------+-----------+
|        NAME         |  STATE  | IPV4 | IPV6 |    TYPE    | SNAPSHOTS |
+---------------------+---------+------+------+------------+-----------+
| first-lxd-container | STOPPED |      |      | PERSISTENT | 0         |
+---------------------+---------+------+------+------------+-----------+
$
```

To permanently remove or delete the container, use the following command:

```
$ lxc delete first-lxd-container
$ lxc list
+------+-------+------+------+------+-----------+
| NAME | STATE | IPV4 | IPV6 | TYPE | SNAPSHOTS |
+------+-------+------+------+------+-----------+
$
```

# Summary

In this chapter you have created, started, and logged into containers created by each of LXC and LXD. It is easy to create containers using these tools. They are lightweight and easy to use, and you can be up and running in a few seconds. So far, we have just looked at some basic usage of containers to get an operating system working. More advanced usage scenarios will be covered in the coming chapters.

# CHAPTER 4

# LXC and LXD Resources

This chapter discusses the various resources available to create LXC and LXD containers. It explains the internal working of some LXC templates and LXD images with the help of illustrations. LXC installation provides templates that are used to create the containers with various operating system distributions. Each template is a shell script that downloads or bootstraps a minimal system with the basic contents required for container creation using the lxc-create command.

## Default LXC Templates

The lxc-create command takes the template as a parameter using the -t option. We will go through some of the commonly used templates and the options they offer.

The default templates available in a typical LXC installation are as follows:

| | | |
|---|---|---|
| lxc-alpine | lxc-centos | lxc-fedora |
| lxc-oracle | lxc-sshd | lxc-altlinux |
| lxc-cirros | lxc-gentoo | lxc-plamo |
| lxc-ubuntu | lxc-archlinux | lxc-debian |
| lxc-openmandriva | lxc-slackware | lxc-ubuntu-cloud |
| lxc-busybox | lxc-download | lxc-opensuse |
| lxc-sparclinux | | |

The previous chapter introduced some of the template scripts used by LXC to create LXC containers. As you saw, the download template is quite different from the other templates; it uses an image server to provide the basic files to create the containers for different operating system distributions. Other templates do a full distribution bootstrap on the host machine, which is time consuming and depends on the host machine resources. In the following sections let's have a closer look at the working of both the download and distribution specific templates.

## Download Template

The download template provides a way to create containers of different operating system distributions using a common interface. As mentioned, the download template uses an image server to download the initial data required to create the container. The download

© Senthil Kumaran S. 2017
S. Kumaran S., *Practical LXC and LXD*, DOI 10.1007/978-1-4842-3024-4_4

template uses prepackaged, heavily compressed, signed container images available from a central image server such as https://images.linuxcontainers.org/, which provides a faster and much reliable way of container creation. The image server holds image builds of different operating system distributions. The formats of these images are described in the "LXD Image Formats" section later in this chapter.

In host machines with fewer resources, the download template comes in handy because it uses a prebuilt image rather than building the image on the host machine. Building the image involves bootstrapping a minimal rootfs and installing all the basic packages for the requested operating system distribution into the rootfs. Building the image on the host machine can be a time-consuming process if the Internet connection is slow. The download template provides the following options (from the download template --help menu):

```
LXC container image downloader

Special arguments:
[ -h | --help ]: Print this help message and exit.
[ -l | --list ]: List all available images and exit.

Required arguments:
[ -d | --dist <distribution> ]: The name of the distribution
[ -r | --release <release> ]: Release name/version
[ -a | --arch <architecture> ]: Architecture of the container

Optional arguments:
[ --variant <variant> ]: Variant of the image (default: "default")
[ --server <server> ]: Image server (default: "images.linuxcontainers.org")
[ --keyid <keyid> ]: GPG keyid (default: 0x...)
[ --keyserver <keyserver> ]: GPG keyserver to use
[ --no-validate ]: Disable GPG validation (not recommended)
[ --flush-cache ]: Flush the local copy (if present)
[ --force-cache ]: Force the use of the local copy even if expired

LXC internal arguments (do not pass manually!):
[ --name <name> ]: The container name
[ --path <path> ]: The path to the container
[ --rootfs <rootfs> ]: The path to the container's rootfs
[ --mapped-uid <map> ]: A uid map (user namespaces)
[ --mapped-gid <map> ]: A gid map (user namespaces)
```

The following is an example of using the download template to create an Arch Linux-based container:

```
$ sudo lxc-create -t download -n archlinux-test -- --dist archlinux --
release current --arch amd64
Setting up the GPG keyring
Downloading the image index
Downloading the rootfs
```

40

```
Downloading the metadata
The image cache is now ready
Unpacking the rootfs

---

You just created an ArchLinux container (release=current, arch=amd64,
variant=default)

For security reason, container images ship without user accounts
and without a root password.

Use lxc-attach or chroot directly into the rootfs to set a root password
or create user accounts.
$
```

Let's have a closer look at the steps involved in creating the preceding Arch Linux container. The download template does the following:

1.  It downloads the image index from the image server (http://images.linuxcontainers.org/) to determine if the requested distribution with the supplied parameters is available. The index includes basic information about each of the images available, such as the release, architecture, creation timestamp, and the path of the image files within the server. The image index file has lines similar to the one shown here:

    alpine;3.1;amd64;default;20170319_17:50;/images/
    alpine/3.1/amd64/default/20170319_17:50/

    For example, the image file for the requested Arch Linux distribution is available in the server at this path: https://
    images.linuxcontainers.org/images/archlinux/current/
    amd64/default/20170505_01:27/

    This location holds the following files:

    ```
    SHA256SUMS          2017-05-05 04:34      232
    SHA256SUMS.asc      2017-05-05 04:34      819
    lxd.tar.xz          2017-05-05 04:34      604
    lxd.tar.xz.asc      2017-05-05 04:34      819
    meta.tar.xz         2017-05-05 04:34      556
    meta.tar.xz.asc     2017-05-05 04:34      819
    rootfs.tar.xz       2017-05-05 04:34      114M
    rootfs.tar.xz.asc   2017-05-05 04:34      819
    ```

---

■ **Note** The preceding listing may vary, and there is a possibility the link here will break. The server is updated using a build system that truncates irrelevant or old files. This listing is the file listing at the time of writing this chapter.

---

2. The download template then downloads `rootfs.tar.xz` from the image server URL for the specific distribution requested. This provides the specific rootfs for the requested release and architecture of the Arch Linux distribution.

3. After downloading the rootfs, the metadata file is downloaded next. It includes some basic information for setting up the Arch Linux container. The following are the files present in the `meta.tar.xz` file:

```
config  config-user  create-message
excludes-user  expiry templates
```

The contents of the preceding files are as follows:

```
$ cat config
lxc.include = LXC_TEMPLATE_CONFIG/archlinux.common.conf
lxc.arch = x86_64
$ cat config-user
lxc.include = LXC_TEMPLATE_CONFIG/archlinux.common.conf
lxc.include = LXC_TEMPLATE_CONFIG/archlinux.userns.conf
lxc.arch = x86_64
$ cat create-message
You just created an ArchLinux container
(release=current, arch=amd64, variant=default)

For security reason, container images ship without user accounts
and without a root password.

Use lxc-attach or chroot directly into the rootfs to
set a root password
or create user accounts.
$ cat excludes-user

$ cat expiry
1496539775
$ cat templates
/etc/hostname
/etc/hosts
$
```

4.  The preceding files that are downloaded from the image
    server are cached in the /var/cache/lxc/download folder, in
    a separate tree for each of the distributions. The cache will be
    used for any subsequent creation of containers of the same
    type, provided the timestamp in the image server matches or
    expiry is still valid.

5.  The rootfs is extracted to /var/lib/lxc/{container-name},
    where container-name is the name of the container provided
    in the -n option.

6.  Once the rootfs is extracted, a minimal setup of the container
    is done to make it bootable and packages are installed if any
    have been requested.

Thus, a container with the requested distribution, release, and architecture is created
using the download template.

# Distribution-Specific Templates

This section covers the templates for two distributions: Debian and Fedora.

## Debian Template

The Debian template provides the following options, which are quite different from the
options offered by the download template:

The Debian template-specific options can be passed to lxc-create after a -- like
this:

```
lxc-create --name=NAME [-lxc-create-options] -- [-template-options]
```

```
Usage: /usr/share/lxc/templates/lxc-debian -h|--help -p|--path=<path>
[-c|--clean] [-a|--arch=<arch>] [-r|--release=<release>]
                            [--mirror=<mirror>] [--security-
                            mirror=<security mirror>]
                            [--package=<package_name1,package_
                            name2,...>]
```

```
Options :

 -h, --help              print this help text
 -p, --path=PATH         directory where config and rootfs of this VM will be kept
 -a, --arch=ARCH         The container architecture. Can be one of: i686, x86_64,
                         amd64, armhf, armel, powerpc. Defaults to host arch.
 -r, --release=RELEASE   Debian release. Can be one of: wheezy, jessie,
                         stretch, sid.
                         Defaults to current stable.
```

```
--mirror=MIRROR          Debian mirror to use during installation.
                         Overrides the MIRROR
                         environment variable (see below).
--security-mirror=SECURITY_MIRROR
                         Debian mirror to use for security updates.
                         Overrides the
                         SECURITY_MIRROR environment variable (see below).
--packages=PACKAGE_NAME1,PACKAGE_NAME2,...
                         List of additional packages to install. Comma
                         separated, without space.
-c, --clean              only clean up the cache and terminate
--enable-non-free        include also Debian's contrib and non-free
                         repositories.
```

```
Environment variables:

MIRROR                   The Debian package mirror to use. See also the
                         --mirror switch above.
                         Defaults to 'http://httpredir.debian.org/debian'
SECURITY_MIRROR          The Debian package security mirror to use. See also
                         the --security-mirror switch above.
                         Defaults to 'http://security.debian.org/'
```

The following is an example usage of the Debian template to create a Stretch-based container:

```
$ sudo lxc-create -t debian -n stretch-test -- --release stretch --
packages=wget,iputils-ping --mirror=http://deb.debian.org/debian/ --
security-mirror=http://deb.debian.org/debian-security/
debootstrap is /usr/sbin/debootstrap
Checking cache download in /var/cache/lxc/debian/rootfs-stretch-amd64 ...
gpg: keybox '/var/cache/lxc/debian/archive-key.gpg' created
gpg: directory '/home/stylesen/.gnupg' created
gpg: new configuration file '/home/stylesen/.gnupg/dirmngr.conf' created
gpg: new configuration file '/home/stylesen/.gnupg/gpg.conf' created
gpg: /home/stylesen/.gnupg/trustdb.gpg: trustdb created
gpg: key 7638D0442B90D010: public key "Debian Archive Automatic Signing Key
(8/jessie) <ftpmaster@debian.org>" imported
gpg: Total number processed: 1
gpg:               imported: 1
gpg: no ultimately trusted keys found
Downloading debian minimal ...
I: Retrieving InRelease
----------OUTPUT TRUNCATED----------
I: Base system installed successfully.
Download complete.
```

```
Copying rootfs to /var/lib/lxc/stretch-test/rootfs...Generating locales
(this might take a while)...
 en_IN.en_IN...character map file `en_IN' not found: No such file or directory
done
Generation complete.
update-rc.d: error: cannot find a LSB script for checkroot.sh
update-rc.d: error: cannot find a LSB script for umountfs
update-rc.d: error: cannot find a LSB script for hwclockfirst.sh
Creating SSH2 RSA key; this may take some time ...
----------OUTPUT TRUNCATED----------
invoke-rc.d: could not determine current runlevel
invoke-rc.d: policy-rc.d denied execution of start.

Current default time zone: 'Etc/UTC'
Local time is now:      Wed May 24 15:13:39 UTC 2017.
Universal Time is now:  Wed May 24 15:13:39 UTC 2017.

Root password is 'root', please change !
Installing packages: wget iputils-ping
Hit:1 http://deb.debian.org/debian stretch InRelease
----------OUTPUT TRUNCATED----------
Processing triggers for libc-bin (2.24-10) ...
W: --force-yes is deprecated, use one of the options starting with --allow
instead.
$
```

Let's examine the steps involved in creating the preceding Debian container:

1. The Debian template uses debootstrap to create a minimal Debian system with the provided parameters such as release, mirror, and security_mirror. This minimal Debian system is bootstrapped in the folder /var/cache/lxc/debian/, if the requested rootfs is not already available there. The rootfs created in /var/cache/lxc/debian/ is copied to /var/lib/lxc/{container-name}, where container-name is the name of the container passed via the -n option.

2. After copying the rootfs, the Debian template script sets up the basic configuration for the newly created container.

The following are some options that are unique to the Debian templates:

- The option --packages accepts a comma-separated list of packages that should be installed to the newly created container. Once the minimal Debian system rootfs is copied to the container location, the download template script installs the list of packages supplied to the --packages option into the newly created container using apt. This happens before starting the container, as part of container creation itself. It comes in handy when we want to get a container set up with all tools and software packages installed before booting into the container.

- The --mirror and --security-mirror options accept Debian mirror URLs that will be used for downloading any packages needed, whether for the bootstrap or in the list of extra packages requested. Some users may have a local Debian mirror from which they can install the packages instead of wasting Internet bandwidth; otherwise, a user can point to a mirror close to the user's geographical location to expedite the download.

## Fedora Template

The Fedora template provides the following options to create a Fedora-based container:

```
Host CPE ID from /etc/os-release:
usage:
        /usr/share/lxc/templates/lxc-fedora -n|--name=<container_name>
        [-p|--path=<path>] [-c|--clean] [-R|--release=<Fedora_release>]
        [--fqdn=<network name of container>] [-a|--arch=<arch of the container>]
        [--mask-tmp]
        [-h|--help]
Mandatory args:
 -n,--name      container name, used to as an identifier for that container
Optional args:
 -p,--path      path to where the container will be created,
                defaults to /var/lib/lxc.
 --rootfs       path for actual rootfs.
 -c,--clean     clean the cache
 -R,--release   Fedora release for the new container.
                Defaults to host's release if the host is Fedora.
   --fqdn       fully qualified domain name (FQDN) for DNS and system naming
 -a,--arch      Define what arch the container will be [i686,x86_64]
 --mask-tmp     Prevent systemd from over-mounting /tmp with tmpfs.
 -h,--help      print this help
```

The following is an example of using the Fedora template to create a container based on Fedora release 25:

```
$ sudo lxc-create -t fedora -n fedora-test -- --release 25
Host CPE ID from /etc/os-release:
Checking cache download in /var/cache/lxc/fedora/x86_64/25/rootfs ...
Downloading fedora minimal ...
Fetching release rpm name from http://mirror.rise.ph/fedora/linux/releases/25/
Everything/x86_64/os//Packages/f...
 % Total    % Received % Xferd  Average Speed   Time    Time     Time  Current
                                Dload   Upload  Total   Spent    Left  Speed
```

```
----------OUTPUT TRUNCATED----------
Bootstrap Environment testing...

Fedora Installation Bootstrap Build...

Downloading stage 0 LiveOS squashfs file system from archives.fedoraproject.
org...
Have a beer or a cup of coffee.  This will take a bit (~300MB).
----------OUTPUT TRUNCATED----------
Complete!
Fixing up rpm databases
Download complete.
Copy /var/cache/lxc/fedora/x86_64/25/rootfs to /var/lib/lxc/fedora-test/
rootfs ...
Copying rootfs to /var/lib/lxc/fedora-test/rootfs ...
Storing root password in '/var/lib/lxc/fedora-test/tmp_root_pass'
Expiring password for user root.
passwd: Success
installing fedora-release package
Redirecting to '/usr/bin/dnf -y install fedora-release' (see 'man yum2dnf')

Failed to set locale, defaulting to C
Fedora 25 - x86_64                             4.7 MB/s | 50 MB       00:10
Fedora 25 - x86_64 - Updates                   2.0 MB/s | 23 MB       00:11
Last metadata expiration check: 0:00:11 ago on Thu May 25 22:59:00 2017.
Package fedora-release-25-2.noarch is already installed, skipping.
Dependencies resolved.
Nothing to do.
Complete!

Container rootfs and config have been created.
Edit the config file to check/enable networking setup.

You have successfully built a Fedora container and cache. This cache may
be used to create future containers of various revisions. The directory
/var/cache/lxc/fedora/x86_64/bootstrap contains a bootstrap
which may no longer needed and can be removed.

A LiveOS directory exists at /var/cache/lxc/fedora/x86_64/LiveOS.
This is only used in the creation of the bootstrap run-time-environment
and may be removed.

The temporary root password is stored in:

        '/var/lib/lxc/fedora-test/tmp_root_pass'
```

The root password is set up as expired and will require it to be changed at first login, which you should do as soon as possible. If you lose the root password or wish to change it without starting the container, you can change it from the host by running the following command (which will also reset the expired flag):

```
chroot /var/lib/lxc/fedora-test/rootfs passwd
```

$

The following steps are involved in creating the preceding Fedora container:

1. The Fedora template downloads a minimal Fedora system with the provided parameters such as release. This minimal Fedora system is created in the folder /var/cache/lxc/fedora/, if the requested rootfs is not already there.

2. Inside this minimal Fedora system, the required Fedora mirrors are set up and the basic software packages are installed using yum package manager.

3. The rootfs created in /var/cache/lxc/fedora/ is copied to /var/lib/lxc/{container-name}, where container-name is the name of the container passed via the -n option.

4. After copying the rootfs, the Fedora template script sets up the basic configuration for the newly created container. The template also generates a root password and copies it to a specific location within the container directory.

---

■ **Note** To see the different options provided by any of the LXC template scripts, use the following command (where {name} is the name of the template):

```
$ /usr/share/lxc/templates/lxc-{name} --help
```

All the LXC template scripts use /var/cache/lxc/ as the cache folder in order to store the minimal bootstrapped rootfs of the different distributions. Subsequent lxc-create commands to create a container that is already available from the cache use the rootfs from the cache instead of downloading everything from the Internet, making the creation faster. Each template uses a different invalidation mechanism for the cache.

---

# LXD Images

LXD uses images to create containers and has no other mechanism, unlike LXC. LXD uses the same image server as the download template to provide an image-based workflow, with advanced caching and preloading support to keep the images up to date in the host machine's cache. The containers created by LXD are created from images obtained from image servers or locally created images with a specific format.

## LXD Image Formats

LXD image formats are easy to understand. Standard contents of an LXD image format are as follows:

- Container filesystem
- Metadata file, which describes
  - When the image was made
  - When the image expires
  - What architecture the image supports
- Optionally, a bunch of file templates, used for configuring the container

LXD supports two image formats:

- Unified image (single tarball)
- Split image (two tarballs)

---

■ **Note**    LXD is used for OS-based containers and has nothing to do with application containers. Hence, LXD does not support any of the application container–specific standard image formats available as of this writing. In other words, LXD does not support either Docker image formats or other virtual machine image formats.

---

## Unified Image

The unified image format is a single tarball that is self-contained with all the files required to support an LXD image. This is the format used for officially supplied LXD images in the past (now the official images are split images, as explained in the following section). The tarball may be either compressed or uncompressed. The SHA256 checksum of the image tarball is used as the image identifier.

The contents of the unified image tarball are as follows:

- `rootfs/`

- `metadata.yaml`

- `templates/` (optional)

A typical `metadata.yaml` file looks something like this:

```
architecture: "x86_64"
creation_date: 1495726848
properties:
        architecture: "x86_64"
        description: "Ubuntu 16.04 LTS server (20170525)"
        os: "ubuntu"
        release: "xenial"
templates:
        /etc/hostname:
        when:
        - create
        - copy
        template: hostname.tpl
        /var/lib/cloud/seed/nocloud-net/meta-data:
        when:
        - create
        - copy
        template: cloud-init-meta.tpl
        /var/lib/cloud/seed/nocloud-net/network-config:
        when:
        - create
        - copy
        template: cloud-init-network.tpl
        /var/lib/cloud/seed/nocloud-net/user-data:
        when:
        - create
        - copy
        template: cloud-init-user.tpl
        properties:
        default: |
                #cloud-config
                {}
        /var/lib/cloud/seed/nocloud-net/vendor-data:
        when:
        - create
        - copy
        template: cloud-init-vendor.tpl
```

```
properties:
default: |
        #cloud-config
        {}
/etc/init/console.override:
when:
- create
template: upstart-override.tpl
/etc/init/tty1.override:
when:
- create
template: upstart-override.tpl
/etc/init/tty2.override:
when:
- create
template: upstart-override.tpl
/etc/init/tty3.override:
when:
- create
template: upstart-override.tpl
/etc/init/tty4.override:
when:
- create
template: upstart-override.tpl
```

This metadata.yaml files has two mandatory fields, architecture and creation_date. The architecture field specifies the architecture to which the image applies, and the creation_date field specifies the date of creation of the image in UNIX time_t format. The other extra properties available in the metadata file are there for the convenience of the user; they give a detailed description of the image. These extra properties are used by commands such as lxc image list and to perform a key/value search for a particular image. These extra properties can be edited by the users with the help of the lxc image edit command, though the architecture and creation_date fields are immutable.

---

■ **Note**    UNIX time_t (also known as POSIX time) is a system for describing instants in time, defined as the number of seconds that have elapsed since 00:00:00 Coordinated Universal Time (UTC), Thursday, 1 January 1970 (known as the epoch).

---

# Templates

LXD templates use the pongo2 templating engine for the template syntax. The template provides a way to generate or regenerate some files during the lifecycle of a container. In custom images, there can also be custom templates added to change or dynamically

51

configure certain files within the container. The templates found in the metadata.yaml file previously discussed can take one of the following values for the when key:

- create: Run at the time a new container is created from the image
- copy: Run when a container is created from an existing one
- start: Run every time the container is started

The following context is available during the template execution:

- trigger: Name of the event that triggered the template
- path: Path of the file being templated
- container: Key/value map of container properties (name, architecture, privileged, and ephemeral)
- config: Key/value map of the container's configuration
- devices: Key/value map of the devices assigned to this container
- properties: Key/value map of the template properties specified in metadata.yaml

---

■ **Note**    pongo2 is the successor to pongo, a Django syntax–like templating language. The project is available from https://github.com/flosch/pongo2

---

## Split Image

The split image format has two distinct tarballs, one for the rootfs and the other for metadata. The metadata file contains the following:

- expiry
- create-message
- templates (optional)
- config-user
- config
- excludes-user

The rootfs tarball simply contains the container root filesystem at its root. A listing of the untarred rootfs.tar file will have the following folders:

```
$ ls
bin   dev   home  lib64  opt   root  sbin  sys  usr
boot  etc   lib   mnt    proc  run   srv   tmp  var
$
```

These two tarballs may be either compressed or uncompressed, and each tarball may choose its own compression algorithm—it is not mandatory to use the same compression algorithm for both the tarballs. This is the current format in which the LXD project officially generates its images at the time of this writing. The image identifier is the SHA256 checksum of the concatenation of the metadata and the rootfs tarball (in that order). For example, to calculate the image identifier, we can use the following command on the metadata and rootfs tarballs:

```
$ cat meta.tar.xz rootfs.tar.xz | sha256sum
119fd125d0c4f67525096aa5d34759cf15971fd667915dd84ad509b3d18c1848   -
$
```

Many operating system distributions provide a rootfs tarball, which can be directly used as the rootfs tarball without any modification. This is the major advantage of the split-image format over the older single-image format.

## Using LXD Images

The images are normally obtained from a remote image server and cached in a local LXD image store, then used to create a container. This means that the first time an image is used, it may take some time to download it, but future uses will typically be much quicker.

The image can be referred to in various different ways on the image server, such as by using the image short hash, full hash, or an alias. Here are some examples of creating a Debian Stretch container by referring to it with different image identifiers:

```
$ sudo lxc launch images:debian/stretch test-container-1
Creating test-container-1
Starting test-container-1
$ sudo lxc launch images:93e45634460f test-container-2
Creating test-container-2
Starting test-container-2
$ sudo lxc launch images:93e45634460fcd6d8107a2d9ddfb06dba18634d134ac26819af
74b33d31add11 test-container-3
Creating test-container-3
Starting test-container-3
$
```

Since the image is cached in the LXD image store locally, we can also launch the container from our local image store as follows:

```
$ sudo lxc launch local:93e45634460f test-container-4
Creating test-container-4
Starting test-container-4
$
```

Or, we can simply do the following, where `local:` is understood if not specified:

```
$ sudo lxc launch 93e45634460f test-container-5
Creating test-container-5
Starting test-container-5
$
```

As we saw previously, LXD caches the image automatically when asked to create a container for the first time from a remote image server. It downloads the image, marks the image as cached, and records the origin of the image. If the image is unused for a period of time (10 days by default), LXD automatically removes the cached image from the local image store. LXD checks for updates to the image on the remote server every 6 hours by default and updates the local cache whenever there is a new version available. All this behavior can be controlled within LXD configuration.

To change from the default of 10 days the number of days before unused images are removed from the local cache, use the following command:

```
$ sudo lxc config set images.remote_cache_expiry 5
```

You can also modify the auto-update interval to check for updates for a new version on the remote server from the default 6 hours to 24 hours with the following command:

```
$ sudo lxc config set images.auto_update_interval 24
```

To update only the cached images on which the `--auto-update` flag is set, use the following command:

```
$ sudo lxc config set images.auto_update_cached false
```

To view the configuration parameters that are set on the local image store/server, use the following command. The configuration parameters we previously set are shown in the following command run:

```
$ sudo lxc config show
config:
 core.https_address: '[::]:8443'
 images.auto_update_cached: "false"
 images.auto_update_interval: "24"
 images.remote_cache_expiry: "5"
$
```

# Copying Images

LXD provides a way to copy an image from a remote image server to the local image store without creating or launching a container immediately. The copied image can be used later to create a container—this is useful when you want to cache certain images when you have an Internet connection and later use these cached images to create containers when disconnected from the Internet.

```
$ sudo lxc image copy images:debian/jessie local:
Image copied successfully!
$
$ sudo lxc image list
+-------+--------------+------+-------------+------+--------+---------------+
|ALIAS| FINGERPRINT |PUBLIC| DESCRIPTION | ARCH | SIZE  | UPLOAD DATE   |
+-------+--------------+------+-------------+------+--------+---------------+
|       | 489c3fa793c4| no   |Debian jessie |x86_64| 94.17MB| May 26, 2017  |
                             amd64                    at 9:20am (UTC)
                             (20170504_02:41)
+-------+--------------+------+-------------+------+-------+---------------+
$
```

To save yourself from having to remember the cryptic fingerprint as an image identifier for the copied image in the local image store, you can create an alias while copying the image as follows:

```
$ sudo lxc image copy images:debian/stretch local: --alias debian-stretch
Image copied successfully!
$ sudo lxc image list debian
+---------+--------------+-------+-------------+-------+----v-+-------------+
| ALIAS | FINGERPRINT |PUBLIC| DESCRIPTION | ARCH | SIZE | UPLOAD DATE |
+---------+--------------+-------+-------------+-------+------+-------------+
|debian-| 93e45634460f | no   | Debian stretch | x86_64|95.98MB| May 26, 2017 |
 stretch                       amd64                     at 9:14am (UTC)
                               (20170504_02:41)
+---------+--------------+-------+-------------+-------+------+-------------+
$
```

# Importing Images

The LXD image formats described previously in the "LXD Image Formats" section can be imported to the local image store using the lxc import command as describe in this section.

To import a single tarball or the unified tarball, with an alias to refer it, use the following command:

```
$ sudo lxc image import xenial-server-cloudimg-amd64-lxd.tar.xz --alias
custom-xenial
Image imported with fingerprint: a1fca7830c07fb024fa246fb02798e3627caafd793b
ba81397e6a7bd8b5f547e
$ sudo lxc image list
```

```
+--------+--------------+--------+-------------+------+------+-------------+
| ALIAS  | FINGERPRINT  | PUBLIC | DESCRIPTION | ARCH | SIZE | UPLOAD DATE |
+--------+--------------+--------+-------------+------+------+-------------+
|custom- | a1fca7830c07 | no     | Ubuntu 16.04|x86_64|0.00MB| May 26, 2017|
 xenial                           LTS server              at 9:23am (UTC)
                                  (20170525)
+--------+--------------+--------+-------------+------+------+-------------+
$
```

To import split tarballs (i.e., two separate tarballs) with an alias, use the following command:

```
$ sudo lxc image import meta.tar.gz rootfs.tar.xz --alias split-xenial
Image imported with fingerprint: e127122143e88dd7f18eae7e60cfecdc6f0c4fc5b4
69689def6f4a0c70fab0d7
$ sudo lxc image list
+--------+--------------+--------+-------------+-------+-------+--------------+
| ALIAS  | FINGERPRINT  | PUBLIC |  DESCRIPTION | ARCH |SIZE   | UPLOAD DATE  |
+--------+--------------+--------+-------------+-------+-------+--------------+
| split  | e127122143e8 | no     | Ubuntu 16.04|x86_64|81.93MB|May 26, 2017  |
 -xenial                          LTS server              at 9:30am (UTC)
                                  (20170525)
+--------+--------------+--------+-------------+-------+-------+--------------+
$
```

## Viewing and Editing Image Information

To get detailed information about an image, use the following command:

```
$ sudo lxc image info ubuntu:16.04
Fingerprint: 8fa08537ae51c880966626561987153e72d073cbe19dfe5abc062713d929254d
Size: 153.70MB
Architecture: x86_64
Public: yes
Timestamps:
        Created: 2017/05/16 00:00 UTC
        Uploaded: 2017/05/16 00:00 UTC
        Expires: 2021/04/21 00:00 UTC
        Last used: never
Properties:
        description: ubuntu 16.04 LTS amd64 (release) (20170516)
        os: ubuntu
        release: xenial
        version: 16.04
        architecture: amd64
        label: release
        serial: 20170516
```

```
Aliases:
        - 16.04
        - 16.04/amd64
        - default
        - default/amd64
        - lts
        - lts/amd64
        - x
        - x/amd64
        - xenial
        - xenial/amd64
Auto update: disabled
$
```

The lxc image edit command allows you to edit this image information with the help of a text editor that will pop up when the command is issued:

```
$ sudo lxc image edit split-xenial
```

---

■ **Note**   In the preceding command, you can refer to an image with either the alias or the fingerprint.

---

The contents shown for editing inside the text editor will look like the following:

```
### This is a yaml representation of the image properties.
### Any line starting with a '# will be ignored.
###
### Each property is represented by a single line:
### An example would be:
###   description: My custom image

auto_update: false
properties:
 architecture: x86_64
 description: Ubuntu 16.04 LTS server (20170525)
 os: ubuntu
 release: xenial
public: false
```

## Deleting Images

You can delete images from the image store as follows:

```
$ sudo lxc image delete 3e50ba589426
```

For the last argument, you can use either the image alias or the fingerprint.

## Exporting Images

If you want to send LXD images to someone else, there is an option to export an image:

```
$ sudo lxc image export split-xenial
Output is in .
$ ls * -alh
-rw------- 1 root root 82M May 26 15:10 e127122143e88dd7f18eae7e60cfecdc6f0c
4fc5b469689def6f4a0c70fab0d7.tar.xz
-rw------- 1 root root 456 May 26 15:10 meta-e127122143e88dd7f18eae7e60cfecd
c6f0c4fc5b469689def6f4a0c70fab0d7.tar.gz
$
```

# Summary

In this chapter, you have seen the various templates of LXC and how they work with some interesting options provided by the templates. LXD works with images that are downloaded from image servers and creates containers using the local cached version of the images. You were introduced to the two different image formats supported by LXD, and you also saw how to work with both remote and local image servers.

■ ■ ■

# CHAPTER 5

# Common Virtualization and Orchestration Tools

LXC provides operating system–level containers, as you saw in previous chapters. In this chapter we will look at various tools that may be used for managing LXC containers. Some of the tools that will be discussed here are common tools that work with different containerization and virtualization technologies, but others are specific to LXC. In some sense LXD can be considered as a tool that provides a new user space experience with which to manage LXC.

## libvirt

libvirt is a library that works with many virtualization technologies and provides a common interface to interact with these technologies. libvirt can be used to manage LXC containers in the same way, with the help of the libvirt LXC driver. Installing libvirt in Ubuntu is easy, which you can do with the following command:

```
$ sudo apt install libvirt-bin lxc
```

You can find out the version of the libvirt-bin package that was installed with this command:

```
$ sudo dpkg -s libvirt-bin | grep '^Version:'
Version: 2.5.0-3ubuntu5.1
$
```

At the time of this writing, the version of libvirt-bin available in Ubuntu 17.04 is 2.5.0. The preceding command should also install the LXC driver for libvirt, but you can double-check its installation with the following command:

```
$ /usr/lib/libvirt/libvirt_lxc -h
/usr/lib/libvirt/libvirt_lxc: option requires an argument -- 'h'
```

© Senthil Kumaran S. 2017
S. Kumaran S., *Practical LXC and LXD*, DOI 10.1007/978-1-4842-3024-4_5

```
syntax: /usr/lib/libvirt/libvirt_lxc [OPTIONS]
```

```
Options

 -b, --background
 -n NAME, --name NAME
 -c FD, --console FD
 -v VETH, --veth VETH
 -s FD, --handshakefd FD
 -S NAME, --security NAME
 -N FD, --share-net FD
 -I FD, --share-ipc FD
 -U FD, --share-uts FD
 -h, --help

$
```

As noted, libvirt is a library to manage virtual machines or containers based on the different drivers available in the libvirt library. Many command-line tools use libvirt. One such tool is `virsh`, which you can use to manage LXC using the hypervisor connection URI argument as `lxc:///`—that is, `virsh -c lxc:///`. Instead of passing the `-c` option to every `virsh` command, you can set the `LIBVIRT_DEFAULT_URI` environment variable to `lxc:///` to use LXC as the default connection URI.

libvirt takes an XML definition in order to manage containers or virtual machines. Let's create a simple XML definition for our container that will be managed by libvirt. The XML definition will look like the following:

```
$ cat lxc-vm1.xml
<domain type='lxc'>
 <name>lxc-vm1</name>
 <memory>1048576</memory>
 <os>
   <type>exe</type>
   <init>/sbin/init</init>
 </os>
 <vcpu>1</vcpu>
 <clock offset='utc'/>
 <on_poweroff>destroy</on_poweroff>
 <on_reboot>restart</on_reboot>
 <on_crash>destroy</on_crash>
 <devices>
   <emulator>/usr/lib/libvirt/libvirt_lxc</emulator>
   <filesystem type='mount'>
     <source dir='/var/lib/lxc/lxc-vm1/rootfs'/>
     <target dir='/'/>
   </filesystem>
```

```
  <interface type='network'>
    <source network='default'/>
  </interface>
  <console type='pty'/>
 </devices>
</domain>
```

This XML configuration document can be used to create a domain in libvirt and save it to disk:

```
$ sudo virsh -c lxc:/// define lxc-vm1.xml
Domain lxc-vm1 defined from lxc-vm1.xml
```

The stored XML configuration can be viewed as follows:

```
$ sudo virsh -c lxc:// dumpxml lxc-vm1
<domain type='lxc'>
 <name>lxc-vm1</name>
 <uuid>232530c7-2ddf-40d5-9082-670dfd87b2b3</uuid>
 <memory unit='KiB'>1048576</memory>
 <currentMemory unit='KiB'>1048576</currentMemory>
 <vcpu placement='static'>1</vcpu>
 <os>
        <type arch='x86_64'>exe</type>
        <init>/sbin/init</init>
 </os>
 <clock offset='utc'/>
 <on_poweroff>destroy</on_poweroff>
 <on_reboot>restart</on_reboot>
 <on_crash>destroy</on_crash>
 <devices>
        <emulator>/usr/lib/libvirt/libvirt_lxc</emulator>
        <filesystem type='mount' accessmode='passthrough'>
        <source dir='/var/lib/lxc/lxc-vm1/rootfs'/>
        <target dir='/'/>
        </filesystem>
        <interface type='network'>
        <mac address='52:54:00:6b:e9:4f'/>
        <source network='default'/>
        </interface>
        <console type='pty'>
        <target type='lxc' port='0'/>
        </console>
 </devices>
</domain>

$
```

61

This XML dump shows some additional parameters that were not defined in our original configuration, such as uuid, currentMemory and unit for memory, mac address, and so forth. These were generated automatically using defaults by virsh define.

Now that the domain is defined, let's create a Debian Stretch–based LXC container, which should have the same name defined in the previous XML configuration (i.e., lxc-vm1):

```
$ sudo lxc-create -t debian -n lxc-vm1 -- --release stretch
```

---

■ **Note**    In the previous chapters, you have seen that by default containers are created inside the directory /var/lib/lxc/{container-name}. This directory should be used in the source dir parameter pointing to the container's rootfs in the XML configuration (with the container-name previously given) using the -n option. There are other methods available to point to the rootfs without using the lxc-create command, which you can explore with the help of libvirt's documentation.

---

Everything required to manage an LXC container is in place, so let's now look at some management commands to manage our newly created LXC container.

## Starting the Container

Use the virsh start command to start the container:

```
$ sudo virsh -c lxc:/// start lxc-vm1
Domain lxc-vm1 started

$
```

Use the virsh list command to see the current state of the container:

```
$ sudo virsh -c lxc:/// list
Id      Name                              State
----------------------------------------------------
22595 lxc-vm1                             running

$
```

## Connecting to the Container Console

To connect to the container started in the previous section, use the virsh connect command as follows:

```
$ sudo virsh -c lxc:/// console lxc-vm1
Connected to domain lxc-vm1
Escape character is ^]
```

```
systemd 232 running in system mode. (+PAM +AUDIT +SELINUX +IMA +APPARMOR +
SMACK +SYSVINIT +UTMP +LIBCRYPTSETUP +GCRYPT +GNUTLS +ACL +XZ +LZ4 +SECCOMP +
BLKID +ELFUTILS +KMOD +IDN)
Detected virtualization lxc-libvirt.
Detected architecture x86-64.

Welcome to Debian GNU/Linux 9 (stretch)!

Set hostname to <lxc-vm1>.
container-getty@3.service: Cannot add dependency job, ignoring: Unit
container-getty@3.service is masked.
container-getty@2.service: Cannot add dependency job, ignoring: Unit
container-getty@2.service is masked.
container-getty@1.service: Cannot add dependency job, ignoring: Unit
container-getty@1.service is masked.
container-getty@0.service: Cannot add dependency job, ignoring: Unit
container-getty@0.service is masked.
container-getty@4.service: Cannot add dependency job, ignoring: Unit
container-getty@4.service is masked.
[  OK  ] Reached target Swap.
[  OK  ] Reached target Remote File Systems.
[  OK  ] Started Forward Password Requests to Wall Directory Watch.
[  OK  ] Listening on Journal Audit Socket.
[  OK  ] Listening on Journal Socket.
[  OK  ] Listening on /dev/initctl Compatibility Named Pipe.
[  OK  ] Listening on Journal Socket (/dev/log).
[  OK  ] Reached target Sockets.
[  OK  ] Created slice System Slice.
----------OUTPUT TRUNCATED----------
[  OK  ] Started Getty on tty1.
[  OK  ] Started Getty on tty3.
[  OK  ] Started Console Getty.
[  OK  ] Started Getty on tty2.
[  OK  ] Started Getty on tty4.
[  OK  ] Reached target Login Prompts.
[  OK  ] Started OpenBSD Secure Shell server.
[  OK  ] Reached target Multi-User System.
         Starting Update UTMP about System Runlevel Changes...
[  OK  ] Started Update UTMP about System Runlevel Changes.

Debian GNU/Linux 9 lxc-vm1 tty1

lxc-vm1 login:
```

If there are multiple consoles in the container, then you can use the following command to connect to different consoles based on the console device name. In LXC, usually console devices are named as console0, console1, console2, and so on.

```
$ sudo virsh -c lxc:/// console lxc-vm1 --devname console0
```

---

■ **Note**　Use ^] or press Ctrl+] to exit from the console, similar to how you exit from a telnet terminal.

---

## Monitoring Container Utilization

You can monitor resource utilization and activities of all the containers on a host using a command called virt-top. This command is not installed by default with libvirt-bin, so you must install it separately as follows:

```
$ sudo apt install virt-top
$ sudo virt-top -c lxc:///
(will open a "top" like interface to show container activities)
$
```

## Rebooting the Container

Use the virsh reboot command as follows to reboot an LXC container. The command first sends a message to the init process via device node /dev/initctl; if this device doesn't exist in the container, then the command sends a SIGHUP to PID 1 inside the LXC container.

```
$ sudo virsh -c lxc:/// reboot lxc-vm1
Domain lxc-vm1 is being rebooted

$
```

## Stopping and Destroying the Container

Use the virsh shutdown command as follows to request a graceful shutdown of the LXC container. The command first sends a message to the init process via device node /dev/initctl, and if such device doesn't exist in the container, then it sends a SIGHTERM to PID 1 inside the LXC container.

```
$ sudo virsh -c lxc:/// shutdown lxc-vm1
Domain lxc-vm1 is being shutdown

$
```

Use the virsh destroy command to forcefully stop the container, if graceful shutdown does not work:

```
$ sudo virsh -c lxc:/// destroy lxc-vm1
Domain lxc-vm1 destroyed

$
```

■ **Note**    The virsh destroy command is used to shut down the container rather than delete or remove the container as in the case of lxc-destroy (covered in Chapter 4).

## Undefining or Deleting a Container from libvirt

To delete or undefine a container from libvirt, use the virsh undefine command:

```
$ sudo virsh -c lxc:/// undefine lxc-vm1
Domain lxc-vm1 has been undefined

$ sudo virsh -c lxc:/// dumpxml lxc-vm1
error: failed to get domain 'lxc-vm1'
error: Domain not found: No domain with matching name 'lxc-vm1'

$
```

■ **Note**    It is recommended to undefine a container after stopping the container. Otherwise, a running container will move from persistent to transient state. Read more about persistent and transient states in the libvirt documentation if you want to know more.

# Virtual Machine Manager GUI

virt-manager is a desktop application to manage virtual machines. It was primarily created for use with KVM, but later support was added for other visualization technologies such as XEN and later containers such as LXC. It can also show the graphical console of the container using the inbuilt VNC or SPICE client viewer, if the container has one. virt-manager uses the libvirt lxc driver to manage LXC containers; hence, installing libvirt-bin is mandatory for managing LXC containers within virt-manager. Install the Virtual Machine Manager desktop application using the following command in Ubuntu:

```
$ sudo apt install virt-manager
```

The Virtual Machine Manager GUI application can be started from the Ubuntu Dash by searching for "virtual" as shown in Figure 5-1.

***Figure 5-1.*** *Searching for Virtual Machine Manager in Ubuntu Dash*

Alternatively, you can open Virtual Machine Manager from the terminal with the following command:

```
$ sudo virt-manager
```

Either way, the application opens a GUI that looks like Figure 5-2.

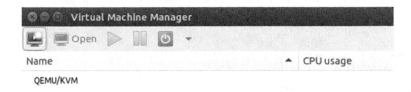

***Figure 5-2.*** *Virtual Machine Manager first screen*

To work with LXC containers in virt-manager, you need to add a new connection type for LXC. The default connection type (as shown in Figure 5-2) is QEMU/KVM. Choose File ➤ Add Connection from the menu, as shown in Figure 5-3.

***Figure 5-3.*** *Choosing to add a connection*

The Add Connection dialog opens, as shown in Figure 5-4.

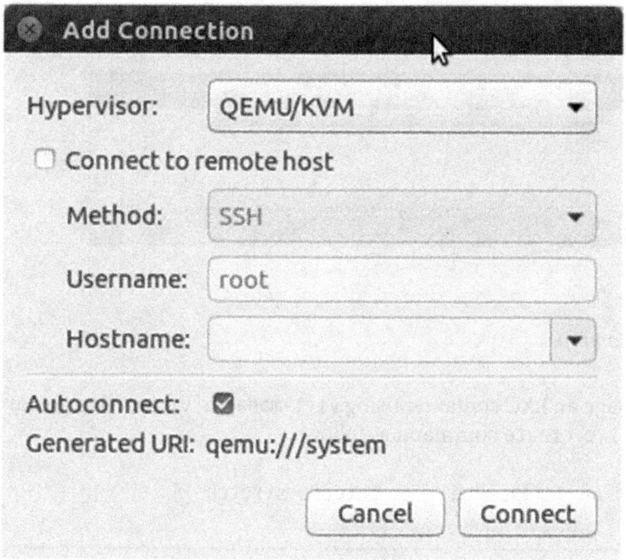

***Figure 5-4.*** *Add Connection dialog*

Then choose the LXC connection Libvirt-LXC (Linux Containers) from the Hypervisor drop-down, as shown in Figure 5-5.

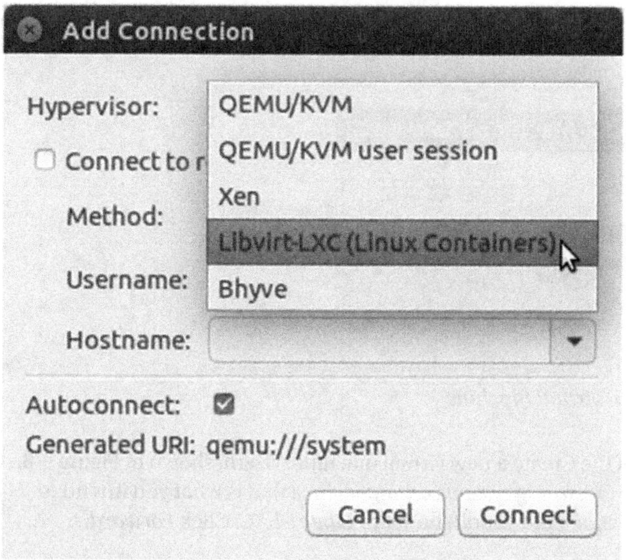

***Figure 5-5.*** *Choosing the LXC connection*

Leave the rest of the settings as they are and click *Connect*. This will list the new connection type that was added in the Virtual Machine Manager application, as shown in Figure 5-6.

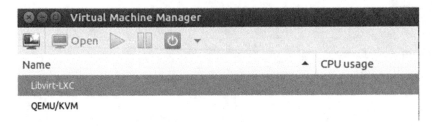

*Figure 5-6. Listing connection types*

Before you start to manage an LXC container using `virt-manager`, you need to create an LXC container using the `lxc-create` command as follows:

```
$ sudo lxc-create -t debian -n lxc-vm1 -- --release stretch
```

---

■ **Note** This is required because `virt-manager` expects an OS directory tree to exist, and creating the OS directory tree is not supported in `virt-manager` yet. This also appears as a warning in the New VM creation screen.

---

Let's create an LXC OS-level container and then manage it using `virt-manager`. Click the *Create a new virtual machine* icon as shown in Figure 5-7.

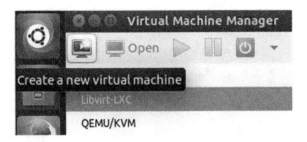

*Figure 5-7. Click Create new virtual machine*

This opens the Step 1 of the Create a new virtual machine wizard, shown in Figure 5-8, in which you should choose *Operating system container* since that is what you intend to create with LXC. The *Connection* field should be set to *Libvirt-LXC*. Click *Forward*.

*Figure 5-8.* *Step 1 of the Create a new virtual machine wizard*

In Step 2 of the Create a new virtual machine wizard, shown in Figure 5-9, provide an existing OS root directory. This is the LXC container that you created already with the lxc-create command prior to launching the wizard. Use the rootfs of this container, which will get created by default in /var/lib/lxc/{container-name}/rootfs as shown in Figure 5-9. Click *Forward*.

*Figure 5-9.* *Step 2 of the Create a new virtual machine wizard*

In Step 3 of the Create a new virtual machine wizard, provide the values for memory and CPU that should be used by the LXC container. The maximum allowed value is shown in Figure 5-10. Click *Forward*.

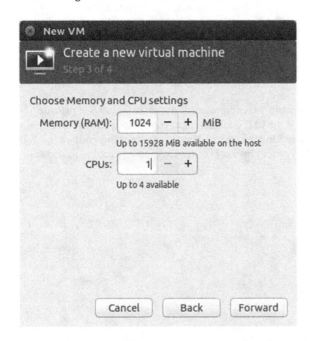

*Figure 5-10.* *Step 3 of the Create a new virtual machine wizard*

In Step 4 of the Create a new virtual machine wizard, shown in Figure 5-11, name the container and choose the network setup. The default NAT network should work in most cases.

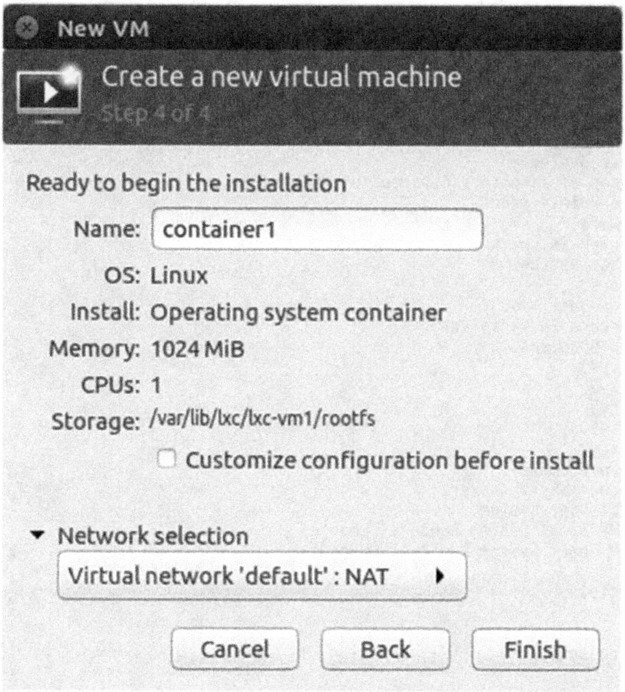

*Figure 5-11. Step 4 of the Create a new virtual machine wizard*

Click *Finish* to begin creation of the container within virt-manager, shown in progress in Figure 5-12.

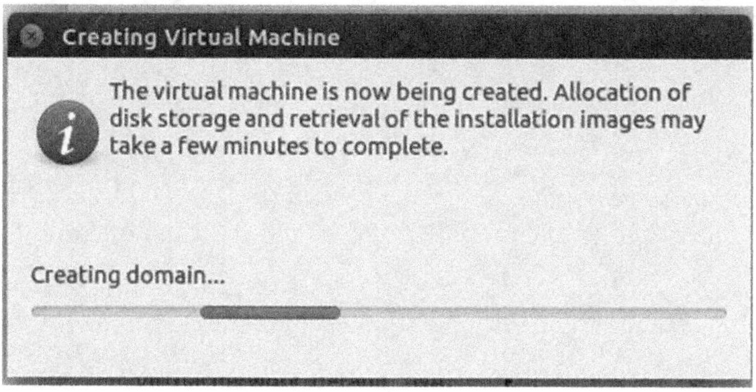

*Figure 5-12. Creating the virtual machine*

After creating the container, virt-manager brings up the console of the container in a separate window. You can use this console to interact with the container, as shown in Figure 5-13.

**Figure 5-13.** *Container console*

Figure 5-14, shows the overview of the container that was just created in virt-manager. Click other navigation menu items such as Performance, CPUs, Memory, Boot Options, NIC, Console1, and Filesystem to get detailed information on other parameters of the container.

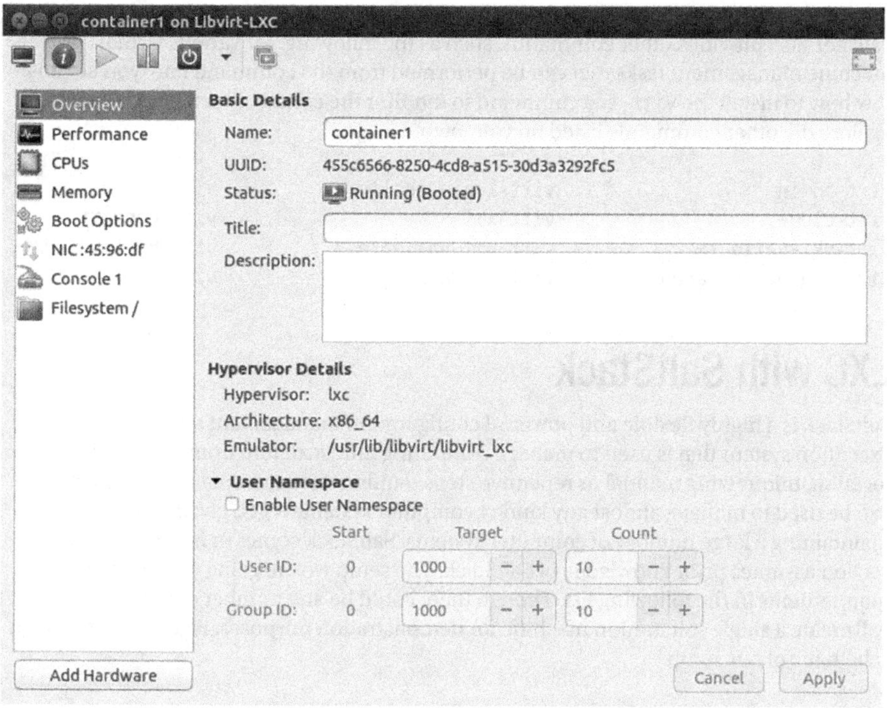

**Figure 5-14.** *Container overview*

The container will be listed in the virt-manager GUI as shown in Figure 5-15, which provides a convenient way of managing the container.

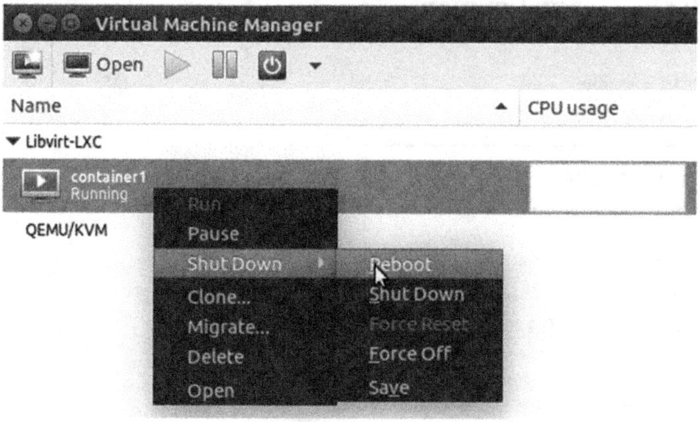

**Figure 5-15.** *List container*

The GUI of Virtual Machine Manager is quite simple and easy to follow. `virt-manager` also provides other commands, such as the following, for various virtual machine management tasks that can be performed from the command line; you already saw how to install the `virt-top` command to monitor the container activities. You can explore the other commands listed on your own.

| | | |
|---|---|---|
| `virt-admin` | `virt-login-shell` | `virt-viewer` |
| `virt-clone` | `virt-xml` | `virt-convert` |
| `virt-pki-validate` | `virt-xml-validate` | `virt-host-validate` |
| `virt-sanlock-cleanup` | `virt-install` | `virt-top` |

# LXC with SaltStack

SaltStack is a highly flexible and powerful configuration management and remote execution system that is used to manage computing infrastructure from a centralized location, minimizing manual or repetitive steps required for maintenance. SaltStack can be used to manage almost any kind of computer system. When given a task of maintaining a large number of computer systems, SaltStack comes in handy. This section assumes prior knowledge of SaltStack. The setup we are going to create has the requirements in the following list. Though there could be any number of minions, we will create a single salt minion machine for demonstration purposes. Figure 5-16 shows a schematic of our setup.

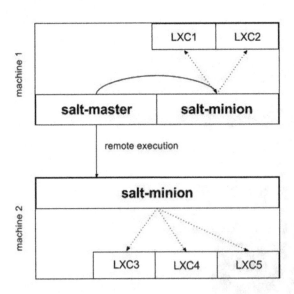

***Figure 5-16.*** *SaltStack setup schematic*

- Configure machine 1 as the salt master server.

- Configure machine 2 as the salt minion.

- Create two LXC containers on machine 1 with the help of salt, since salt master is also a minion.

- Create three LXC containers on machine 2 with the help of salt.

---

■ **Note**    Both the machines, salt master and salt minion, use Ubuntu Server 17.04 (Zesty Zapus) as the operating system.

---

## Salt Master Setup

We will start with setting up the salt master server. In my local network, the salt master machine has Ubuntu Server 17.04 installed and has an IP address of 192.168.1.9, which will be used to communicate with the machine. Log in to the machine that will be used as the salt master server and install SaltStack—both salt master and salt minion daemon packages, as shown here:

```
stylesen@salt-master:~$ sudo apt install salt-master salt-minion salt-ssh
salt-cloud
```

---

■ **Note**    The salt master server we are setting up will also act as a salt minion, so that we can control the salt master server with SaltStack.

---

Create the necessary directories in the default location where salt looks for various files:

```
stylesen@salt-master:~$ sudo mkdir -p /srv/salt
stylesen@salt-master:~$ sudo mkdir -p /srv/formulas
stylesen@salt-master:~$ sudo mkdir -p /srv/pillar
```

Open the file /etc/salt/master and add the following content to the end of the file:

```
file_roots:
 base:
        - /srv/salt
        - /srv/formulas

pillar_roots:
 base:
        - /srv/pillar
```

> ■ **Note** The configuration file /etc/salt/master is written in YAML, so be careful not to mix spaces and tabs, and also be consistent with indentation.

In the preceding configuration, base specifies the default environment. The file_roots section is defined first, which specifies the location where salt master will look for configuration management instructions. Similarly, the pillar_roots section specifies the directory for pillar configurations.

## Minion Configuration

Since the master will also act as a minion, we will also set up minion configuration on the master server. To do this, edit the file /etc/salt/minion and add the following content to the end of the file:

```
master: 127.0.0.1
```

This specifies that the salt master server for this minion is itself, since the minion and master exist in the same machine.

## Restart Daemons

After you have completed all of the preceding setup, restart the daemons to apply the new configuration changes:

```
stylesen@salt-master:~$ sudo service salt-master restart
stylesen@salt-master:~$ sudo service salt-minion restart
```

## Accept Minion Key

We need to verify and accept the minion key for the minion that is running in this (master) machine. List all the keys that salt master knows:

```
stylesen@salt-master:~$ sudo salt-key --list all
Accepted Keys:
Denied Keys:
Unaccepted Keys:
salt-master
Rejected Keys:
stylesen@salt-master:~$
```

The rejected key shown in the previous line is that of the salt minion labeled salt-master, which is the hostname of the master machine. Now, manually verify the fingerprint of both the minion and the salt-master as follows:

```
stylesen@salt-master:~$ sudo salt-call key.finger --local
local:
        e5:89:95:ca:7b:c1:ed:80:09:4a:32:e1:9b:1f:c7:47:05:ab:c2:de:a0:d3:
        c0:0e:f9:80:fa:1d:b0:25:c4:c3
stylesen@salt-master:~$ sudo salt-key -f salt-master
Unaccepted Keys:
salt-master:  e5:89:95:ca:7b:c1:ed:80:09:4a:32:e1:9b:1f:c7:47:05:ab:c2:de:
a0:d3:c0:0e:f9:80:fa:1d:b0:25:c4:c3
stylesen@salt-master:~$
```

Once you have verified that the keys match, mark them as accepted:

```
stylesen@salt-master:~$ sudo salt-key -a salt-master
The following keys are going to be accepted:
Unaccepted Keys:
salt-master
Proceed? [n/Y] y
Key for minion salt-master accepted.
stylesen@salt-master:~$ sudo salt-key --list all
Accepted Keys:
salt-master
Denied Keys:
Unaccepted Keys:
Rejected Keys:
stylesen@salt-master:~$
```

Test if the setup is working fine, using the salt test.ping module as follows:

```
stylesen@salt-master:~$ sudo salt '*' test.ping
salt-master:
        True
stylesen@salt-master:~$
```

The salt master server setup is complete now, with a salt minion running in the same machine.

# Remote Salt Minion Setup

The remote salt minion setup is similar to the setup of the local one demonstrated in the previous section, with the obvious slight difference that it is being done on a different machine. In my local network, the salt minion machine has an IP address of 192.168.1.7, which will be used to communicate with the machine. Log in to the remote machine and install the salt minion daemon as shown here:

```
stylesen@salt-minion:~$ sudo apt install salt-minion
```

Once the salt-minion package is installed, we will again verify the fingerprints manually. Log in to the salt master machine and get the keys; we will specifically need the value for master.pub:

```
stylesen@salt-master:~$ sudo salt-key -F master
Local Keys:
master.pem:   49:07:9e:6a:d3:ed:47:98:46:6a:e7:a0:02:5e:60:e9:35:43:3c:c8:
              95:5d:77:f8:4d:bd:e6:9d:b2:ef:ea:36
master.pub:   b5:61:ed:2f:fe:6e:f9:53:d0:57:a7:fa:7a:57:68:cb:6e:74:04:37:
              ab:eb:28:9d:43:43:ed:f4:52:ee:ec:ec
Accepted Keys:
salt-master:  e5:89:95:ca:7b:c1:ed:80:09:4a:32:e1:9b:1f:c7:47:05:ab:c2:de:
              a0:d3:c0:0e:f9:80:fa:1d:b0:25:c4:c3
stylesen@salt-master:~$
```

In the salt-minion machine, modify the minion configuration file /etc/salt/ minion and add the following content toward the end of the file:

```
master: 192.168.1.9
master_finger: 5:61:ed:2f:fe:6e:f9:53:d0:57:a7:fa:7a:57:68:cb:6e:74:04:37:a
b:e\
b:28:9d:43:43:ed:f4:52:ee:ec:ec
```

Change the IP address of the salt master server from 192.168.1.9 to the appropriate value within your network. master_finger is the value of master.pub obtained from salt master.

After you have made the preceding configuration changes, restart the salt minion daemon as follows:

```
stylesen@salt-minion:~$ sudo service salt-minion restart
```

## Accept Minion Key

The minion should now contact the salt master to send its key for the master to accept. This is done with the following command:

```
stylesen@salt-minion:~$ sudo salt-call key.finger --local
local:
        f8:2c:c5:b3:b6:52:37:68:de:b5:5f:25:f6:70:a7:1b:91:2a:16:a4:e9:43:56:
        d7:54:dd:bb:33:c2:f4:16:95
stylesen@salt-minion:~$
```

On the salt master machine, list the keys, manually verify the fingerprint, and then accept the keys as follows:

```
stylesen@salt-master:~$ sudo salt-key --list all
Accepted Keys:
salt-master
Denied Keys:
Unaccepted Keys:
salt-minion
Rejected Keys:
stylesen@salt-master:~$ sudo salt-key -f salt-minion
Unaccepted Keys:
salt-minion:  f8:2c:c5:b3:b6:52:37:68:de:b5:5f:25:f6:70:a7:1b:91:2a:16:a4:e9:
43:56:d7:54:dd:bb:33:c2:f4:16:95
stylesen@salt-master:~$ sudo salt-key -a salt-minion
The following keys are going to be accepted:
Unaccepted Keys:
salt-minion
Proceed? [n/Y] y
Key for minion salt-minion accepted.
stylesen@salt-master:~$ sudo salt-key -a salt-minion
The following keys are going to be accepted:
Unaccepted Keys:
salt-minion
Proceed? [n/Y] y
Key for minion salt-minion accepted.
stylesen@salt-master:~$ sudo salt-key --list all
Accepted Keys:
salt-master
salt-minion
Denied Keys:
Unaccepted Keys:
Rejected Keys:
stylesen@salt-master:~$
```

Test sending to the minions with the following command:

```
stylesen@salt-master:~$ sudo salt '*' test.ping
salt-minion:
        True
salt-master:
        True
stylesen@salt-master:~$
```

Thus, we have the second minion set up successfully. We will move on to see how to create LXC containers on the minions with the help of SaltStack.

## Salt LXC Management

We must create profiles in order to create LXC containers in the minions. Profiles are configurations defined in either master or minion config files.

---

■ **Note**    This section assumes LXC is already installed in both `salt-master` and `salt-minion` machines. LXC installation is explained in detail in Chapter 2.

---

Let's put a simple container profile in the salt master configuration file /etc/salt/master with the following content. Also there should be a network profile so that the containers get created with networking in place.

```
lxc.container_profile:
 debian_stretch:
        template: debian
        options:
        release: stretch
        arch: amd64
 debian_jessie:
        template: debian
        options:
        release: jessie
        arch: amd64

lxc.network_profile:
 debian_stretch:
        eth0:
        link: virbr0
        type: veth
        flags: up
 debian_jessie:
        eth0:
        link: virbr0
        type: veth
        flags: up
```

With the preceding configuration in place, let's create our two containers in the salt-master machine as planned with the following command:

```
stylesen@salt-master:~$ sudo salt salt-master lxc.create container1
profile=debian_stretch template=debian network_profile=debian_stretch
salt-master:
        ----------
        result:
        True
```

```
        state:
        ----------
        new:
        stopped
        old:
        None
stylesen@salt-master:~$
```

The second container may be cloned from the first container as follows:

```
stylesen@salt-master:~$ sudo salt salt-master lxc.clone container2
orig=container1
salt-master:
        ----------
        result:
        True
        state:
        ----------
        new:
        stopped
        old:
        None
stylesen@salt-master:~$
```

We can now see if the container exists using the lxc-ls command on the salt master server:

```
stylesen@salt-master:~$ sudo lxc-ls --fancy
NAME      STATE    AUTOSTART GROUPS IPV4 IPV6
container1 STOPPED 0          -       -      -
container2 STOPPED 0          -       -      -
stylesen@salt-master:~$
```

Similarly, let's create three Debian Jessie–based LXC containers on the salt-minion machine by executing salt commands from the salt-master as follows:

```
stylesen@salt-master:~$ sudo salt salt-minion lxc.create container3
profile=debian_jessie template=debian network_profile=debian_jessie
salt-minion:
        ----------
        result:
        True
        state:
        ----------
        new:
        stopped
        old:
        None
```

```
stylesen@salt-master:~$ sudo salt salt-minion lxc.create container4
profile=debian_jessie template=debian network_profile=debian_jessie
salt-minion:
        ----------
        result:
        True
        state:
        ----------
        new:
        stopped
        old:
        None
stylesen@salt-master:~$ sudo salt salt-minion lxc.create container5
profile=debian_jessie template=debian network_profile=debian_jessie
salt-minion:
        ----------
        result:
        True
        state:
        ----------
        new:
        stopped
        old:
        None
stylesen@salt-master:~$
```

We can ensure that the three containers were created on the salt-minion machine by issuing the following command on the salt-minion machine:

```
stylesen@salt-minion:~$ sudo lxc-ls --fancy
NAME      STATE    AUTOSTART GROUPS IPV4 IPV6
container3 STOPPED 0                -    -    -
container4 STOPPED 0                -    -    -
container5 STOPPED 0                -    -    -
stylesen@salt-minion:~$
```

# LXC with Vagrant

Vagrant is a popular virtual machine manager used for managing VirtualBox-based virtual machines. Vagrant has been extended to manage other virtual machines using provider plugins. Vagrant can be used to manage LXC containers using the vagrant-lxc provider plugin, which is available as a package in Ubuntu Zesty. To use the vagrant-lxc provider plugin, install it as follows:

```
$ sudo apt install vagrant-lxc
```

In vagrant terms, a new instance is called a vagrant box. To create a vagrant box, we first need to create a directory where our vagrant box will reside, as shown next. The container itself will still be created in the default location /var/lib/lxc.

```
$ mkdir vagrant-box-holder
$ cd vagrant-box-holder/
$
```

Inside this directory, create a vagrant config file with the name Vagrantfile. Vagrant looks for the config file with the exact name. The contents of the vagrant file are as follows, to create our LXC container:

```
Vagrant.configure(2) do |config|
  config.vm.hostname = "vagrant-debian-jessie-lxc"
  config.vm.box = "debian/jessie64"
  config.vm.box_url = "https://atlas.hashicorp.com/debian/boxes/jessie64"
  config.vm.provider :lxc do |lxc, override|
    lxc.container_name = "vagrant-debian-jessie-lxc"
    lxc.customize 'network.type', 'veth'
    lxc.customize 'network.link', 'lxcbr0'
  end
end
```

Most of the preceding parameters should seem obvious, and will be familiar for any Ruby language developer. Let's see what each parameter does:

- config.vm.hostname defines the hostname of the vagrant box.

- config.vm.box is the box image name that will be downloaded from the box image URL specified in config.vm.box_url.

- All the parameters that start with lxc.* are configuration parameters for the LXC container.

To create the vagrant box of our LXC container via vagrant, cd into the vagrant-box-holder directory where Vagrantfile exists and then run vagrant up as shown here:

```
$ sudo vagrant up
Bringing machine 'default' up with 'lxc' provider...
==> default: Box 'debian/jessie64' could not be found. Attempting to find
and install...
        default: Box Provider: lxc
        default: Box Version: >= 0
==> default: Loading metadata for box 'https://atlas.hashicorp.com/debian/
boxes/jessie64'
        default: URL: https://atlas.hashicorp.com/debian/boxes/jessie64
==> default: Adding box 'debian/jessie64' (v8.7.0) for provider: lxc
        default: Downloading: https://atlas.hashicorp.com/debian/boxes/
        jessie64/versions/8.7.0/providers/lxc.box
```

```
==> default: Successfully added box 'debian/jessie64' (v8.7.0) for 'lxc'!
==> default: Importing base box 'debian/jessie64'...
==> default: Checking if box 'debian/jessie64' is up to date...
==> default: Setting up mount entries for shared folders...
        default: /vagrant => /home/stylesen/vagrant-box-holder
==> default: Starting container...
==> default: Waiting for machine to boot. This may take a few minutes...
        default: SSH address: 10.0.3.188:22
        default: SSH username: vagrant
        default: SSH auth method: private key
        default:
        default: Vagrant insecure key detected. Vagrant will automatically
        replace
        default: this with a newly generated keypair for better security.
        default:
        default: Inserting generated public key within guest...
        default: Removing insecure key from the guest if it's present...
        default: Key inserted! Disconnecting and reconnecting using new SSH
        key...
==> default: Machine booted and ready!
==> default: Setting hostname...
$
```

Thus, the vagrant box is created and started via the LXC provider. We can see the newly created vagrant box as follows:

```
$ sudo lxc-ls --fancy
NAME                       STATE    AUTOSTART GROUPS IPV4            IPV6
vagrant-debian-jessie-lxc RUNNING 0                 -      10.0.3.188 -
$
```

We can log in to the vagrant box using the vagrant way via vagrant ssh as follows:

```
$ sudo vagrant ssh
```

```
The programs included with the Debian GNU/Linux system are free software;
the exact distribution terms for each program are described in the
individual files in /usr/share/doc/*/copyright.

Debian GNU/Linux comes with ABSOLUTELY NO WARRANTY, to the extent
permitted by applicable law.
vagrant@vagrant-debian-jessie-lxc:~$ ls /
bin   dev  home lib64   mnt  proc  run   selinux sys usr    var
boot  etc  lib  media   opt  root  sbin  srv     tmp vagrant
vagrant@vagrant-debian-jessie-lxc:~$
```

lxc-attach should also work:

```
$ sudo lxc-attach -n vagrant-debian-jessie-lxc
root@vagrant-debian-jessie-lxc:/#
```

# LXD-WebGUI

LXD-WebGUI is a lightweight web management interface for LXD written in AngularJS. Due to the way this web GUI is written, it does not require any special application server or database server to run. This allows LXD to be installed and initialized in the same system from which the web GUI will be accessed. Also, LXD should be available over the network.

If you did not previously run sudo lxd init as part of installing LXD, as explained in Chapter 2, then run the following:

```
$ sudo lxd init
Do you want to configure a new storage pool (yes/no) [default=yes]? yes
Name of the new storage pool [default=default]: default
Name of the storage backend to use (dir, lvm) [default=dir]: dir
Would you like LXD to be available over the network (yes/no) [default=no]? yes
Would you like stale cached images to be updated automatically (yes/no)
[default=yes]? yes
Would you like to create a new network bridge (yes/no) [default=yes]? yes
What should the new bridge be called [default=lxdbr0]? lxdbr0
What IPv4 address should be used (CIDR subnet notation, "auto" or "none")
[default=auto]? auto
What IPv6 address should be used (CIDR subnet notation, "auto" or "none")
[default=auto]? auto
LXD has been successfully configured.
$
```

LXD-WebGUI is still in the beta release state. It is unavailable as a native Ubuntu package from the Ubuntu repositories. The following illustrates how to install LXD-WebGUI dependencies using the Node Package Manager (npm) and install LXD-WebGUI itself from its git sources:

Install npm using the following command:

```
$ sudo apt install npm
```

Then install two packages via npm, namely bower and http-server:

```
$ sudo npm install -g bower
npm WARN deprecated bower@1.8.0: ..psst! While Bower is maintained, we
recommend Yarn and Webpack for *new* front-end projects! Yarn's advantage
is security and reliability, and Webpack's is support for both CommonJS and
AMD projects. Currently there's no migration path but we hope you'll help us
figure out one.
```

```
/usr/local/bin/bower -> /usr/local/lib/node_modules/bower/bin/bower
/usr/local/lib
`-- bower@1.8.0
```

```
$ sudo npm install -g http-server
```

Symlink or copy nodejs as node as follows:

```
$ sudo ln -s /usr/bin/nodejs /usr/bin/node
```

Clone the LXD-WebGUI git repository as follows:

```
$ git clone https://github.com/dobin/lxd-webgui.git lxd-webgui.git
$ cd lxd-webgui.git/
```

---

■ **Note**    git is a distributed version control system. Install git using the following command if you have not installed it previously:

```
$ sudo apt install git-all
```

---

Install all the web dependencies for LXD-WebGUI using bower (installed previously using npm):

```
$ bower install
bower not-cached       https://github.com/angular/bower-angular.git#~1.4.0
bower resolve          https://github.com/angular/bower-angular.git#~1.4.0
----------OUTPUT TRUNCATED----------
Unable to find a suitable version for angular, please choose one by typing
one of the numbers below:
        1) angular#1.4.14 which resolved to 1.4.14 and is required by
           angular-loader#1.4.14, angular-mocks#1.4.14, angular-route#1.4.14
        2) angular#~1.4.0 which resolved to 1.4.14 and is required by
           angular-seed
        3) angular#^1.2 which resolved to 1.4.14 and is required by
           ng-table#0.8.3
        4) angular#>=1.4.0 which resolved to 1.4.14 and is required by
           angular-bootstrap#1.3.3
        5) angular#>=1.2.18 which resolved to 1.4.14 and is required by
           ui-select#0.16.1
        6) angular#1.6.4 which resolved to 1.6.4 and is required by
           angular-sanitize#1.6.4
```

Prefix the choice with ! to persist it to bower.json

```
? Answer 6
bower install          angular-mocks#1.4.14
bower install          angular-sanitize#1.6.4
bower install          angular-route#1.4.14
bower install          angular-bootstrap#1.3.3
bower install          ui-select#0.16.1
bower install          html5-boilerplate#5.2.0
bower install          angular#1.6.4
bower install          components-font-awesome#4.7.0
bower install          angular-loader#1.4.14
bower install          angular-ui#0.4.0
bower install          ng-table#0.8.3
bower install          bootstrap#3.3.7
bower install          underscore#1.8.3
bower install          jquery#3.2.1


angular-mocks#1.4.14 bower_components/angular-mocks
└── angular#1.6.4


angular-sanitize#1.6.4 bower_components/angular-sanitize
└── angular#1.6.4


angular-route#1.4.14 bower_components/angular-route
└── angular#1.6.4


angular-bootstrap#1.3.3 bower_components/angular-bootstrap
└── angular#1.6.4


ui-select#0.16.1 bower_components/ui-select
└── angular#1.6.4


html5-boilerplate#5.2.0 bower_components/html5-boilerplate


angular#1.6.4 bower_components/angular


components-font-awesome#4.7.0 bower_components/components-font-awesome


angular-loader#1.4.14 bower_components/angular-loader
└── angular#1.6.4


angular-ui#0.4.0 bower_components/angular-ui


ng-table#0.8.3 bower_components/ng-table
└── angular#1.6.4
```

```
bootstrap#3.3.7 bower_components/bootstrap
  └── jquery#3.2.1

underscore#1.8.3 bower_components/underscore

jquery#3.2.1 bower_components/jquery
$
```

Pay attention to the question Prefix the choice with ! to persist it to bower.json? for which we answered 6, which chooses Angular version 1.6.4—the highest and latest version that is shown in the list.

Create an SSL certificate for the http-server and then start the server at port 8000 in order to serve lxd-webgui as follows:

```
$ openssl req -x509 -newkey rsa:2048 -keyout key.pem -out cert.pem -days 365 -nodes
Generating a 2048 bit RSA private key
..........................................++++
.................................................................++++
unable to write 'random state'
writing new private key to 'key.pem'
-----
You are about to be asked to enter information that will be incorporated
into your certificate request.
What you are about to enter is what is called a Distinguished Name or a DN.
There are quite a few fields but you can leave some blank
For some fields there will be a default value,
If you enter '.', the field will be left blank.
-----
Country Name (2 letter code) [AU]:IN
State or Province Name (full name) [Some-State]:TamilNadu
Locality Name (eg, city) []:Chennai
Organization Name (eg, company) [Internet Widgits Pty Ltd]:Linaro Ltd
Organizational Unit Name (eg, section) []:LAVA
Common Name (e.g. server FQDN or YOUR name) []:lxd.stylesen.org
Email Address []:sk@stylesen.org
$ http-server -S -a 0.0.0.0 -p 8000
Starting up http-server, serving ./ through https
Available on:
 https://127.0.0.1:8000
 https://192.168.1.4:8000
Hit CTRL-C to stop the server
```

# LXD Configuration

Begin by creating a self-signed certificate to authenticate to LXD:

```
$ openssl req -x509 -newkey rsa:2048 -keyout key.pem -out cert.pem
-days 365 -nodes
Generating a 2048 bit RSA private key
...............................................................................+++
........+++
unable to write 'random state'
writing new private key to 'key.pem'
-----
You are about to be asked to enter information that will be incorporated
into your certificate request.
What you are about to enter is what is called a Distinguished Name or a DN.
There are quite a few fields but you can leave some blank
For some fields there will be a default value,
If you enter '.', the field will be left blank.
-----
Country Name (2 letter code) [AU]:IN
State or Province Name (full name) [Some-State]:TamilNadu
Locality Name (eg, city) []:Chennai
Organization Name (eg, company) [Internet Widgits Pty Ltd]:Linaro Ltd
Organizational Unit Name (eg, section) []:LAVA
Common Name (e.g. server FQDN or YOUR name) []:lxd-api.stylesen.org
Email Address []:sk@stylesen.org
$
```

Convert the newly created certificate into a PKCS#12 certificate that could be loaded as a client certificate in the user's web browser:

```
$ openssl pkcs12 -export -out cert.p12 -inkey key.pem -in cert.pem
Enter Export Password:
Verifying - Enter Export Password:
$
```

---

■ **Note**    During the execution of the preceding command, if you receive an error stating
unable to write 'random state', issue the following command to remove the .rnd
file created by root and then rerun the preceding command to generate PKCS#12 client
certificate:

```
$ sudo rm ~/.rnd
```

---

The PKCS#12 client certificate is now generated as the file cert.p12 in the current directory. The following list shows how to load the client certificate in Chrome and Firefox:

- *In Chrome*: Click the icon with three vertical dots in the upper-right corner, choose *Settings*, click *Advanced* at the bottom of the page, click *Manage certificates*, click *Import*, click *Next* to launch the Certificate Import Wizard, click *Browse*, and select the cert.p12 certificate.

- *In Firefox*: Choose *Preferences* from Edit menu, click *Advanced* on the left side menu, click *Certificates* tab on the page, click *View Certificates* to launch the Certificate Manager wizard, click *Import* and then select the cert.p12 certificate.

---

■ **Note**    If you are prompted for a password during the certificate import, then supply the same Export Password that you provided during the previous client certificate creation.

---

Now we need to add the cert.pem client certificate generated in the same directory as trusted certificates of LXD, which is done as follows:

```
$ sudo lxc config trust add cert.pem
```

The following commands are used to configure LXD to listen on port 9000 and allow access from localhost port 8000 where the lxd-webgui runs and also some HTTP-specific configuration to run LXD API server:

```
$ sudo lxc config set core.https_address 0.0.0.0:9000
$ sudo lxc config set core.https_allowed_methods "GET, POST, PUT, DELETE, OPTIONS"
$ sudo lxc config set core.https_allowed_headers "Origin, X-Requested-With, Content-Type, Accept"
$ sudo lxc config set core.https_allowed_credentials "true"
$ sudo lxc config set core.https_allowed_origin "*"
$ sudo service lxd restart
```

Now the LXD API server will listen on port 9000, which can be verified as follows:

```
$ netstat -ant | grep 9000
tcp6    0       0 :::9000              :::*              LISTEN
$
```

Access the LXD API server from your web browser with the correct IP address and port, or https://localhost:9000/ if it is served from the same machine, and select the certificate with which you want to authenticate yourself and then click OK as shown in Figure 5-17.

*Figure 5-17.* *Select client certificate*

Once the certificate warning is accepted, the LXD API server responds as shown in Figure 5-18.

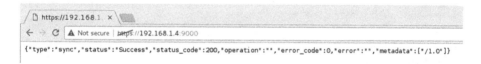

*Figure 5-18.* *LXD API server response*

## NEED FOR THE CERTIFICATES

The following list explains the need for the certificates:

- LXD provides a REST-based API via the HTTPS web server that is available via port 9000, which needs a server certificate.

- The LXD-WebGUI is served via HTTPS via a web server that is available via port 8000, which needs a server certificate too.

- Authentication to the LXD API is performed via a client certificate, which is stored in the web browser of the user. LXD-WebGUI sends HTTP requests to the LXD API server, which should also be authenticated via this client certificate.

# Using LXD-WebGUI

Now we are all set to access our LXD-WebGUI, which is hosted at port 8000. The Settings page shown in Figure 5-19 opens when we access LXD-WebGUI server.

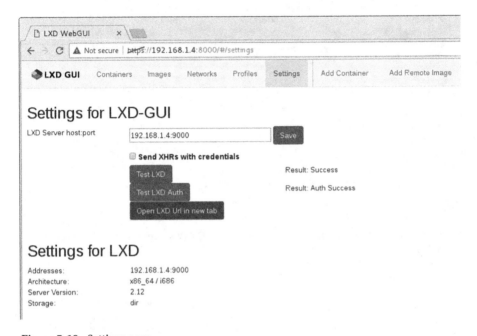

*Figure 5-19. Settings page*

---

**■ Note**    Uncheck *Send XHRs with credentials* if there is a connection error to the LXD API server, especially when you are accessing it from a different machine via an IP address other than localhost. Read more about XHR here: https://developer.mozilla.org/en-US/docs/Web/API/XMLHttpRequest/withCredentials.

---

Let's create a new container using the LXD-WebGUI. Before creating the container, check out Figure 5-20 to see the images available in this LXD server.

*Figure 5-20.* *Available images in LXD server*

---

■ **Note**    The available images shown in Figure 5-20 are the ones that are copied to the local: image server. See the "Importing Images" section in Chapter 4 for details.

---

Let's create a Debian Stretch–based container using lxd-webgui, for which we need to go to the *Add Container* page, as shown in Figure 5-21.

*Figure 5-21.* *Add Container page*

Click the *Add Container* button, and the container will be created immediately and listed on the *Containers* page. The container will be added in the Stopped state, as shown in Figure 5-22.

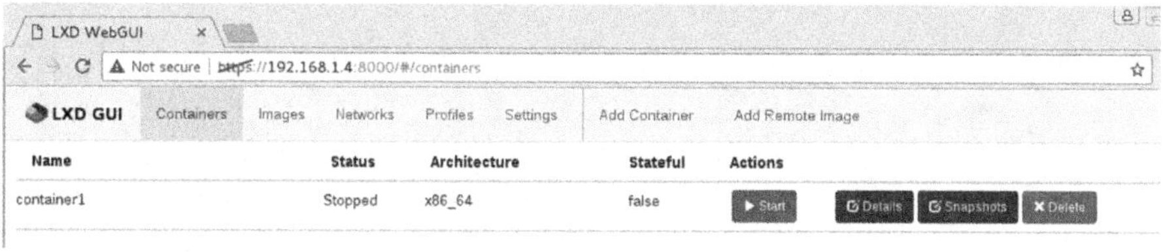

*Figure 5-22.* *Containers list*

Click the *Start* button in the Actions column for the specific container to start running the container. Once the container starts running, we can get access to the container's console right in the web page, as shown in Figure 5-23.

**Figure 5-23.** *Running Container*

Click the *Details* button to get more information about the container, as shown in Figure 5-24.

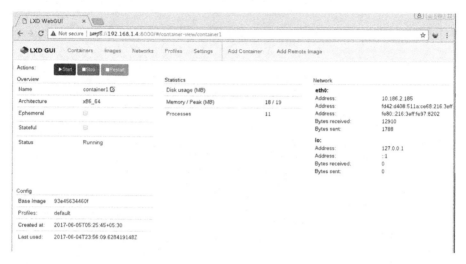

***Figure 5-24.*** *Container details*

The LXD-WebGUI provides a lightweight, easy-to-use GUI for managing LXD containers.

# Summary

Containers are similar to virtualization; many of the common virtualization management tools are capable of handling containers. It becomes important to use a management tool when you need to handle huge swarms of containers. This chapter introduced just a few management and orchestration tools, though there are many available. Almost all modern orchestration tools such as Ansible, Puppet, and so on provide LXC integration in the form of plugins. Users who are already comfortable with particular management or orchestration tools can continue to use them to manage containers without any difficulties.

# CHAPTER 6

■ ■ ■

# Use Cases

Learning about a new technology is a worthwhile pursuit, but to fully comprehend that technology, you need to put it to use. Now that you have a solid understanding of LXC and LXD from the previous chapters, this chapter suggests some use cases that you can follow to apply LXC and LXD in practice. Naturally, there are many possible applications for LXC and LXD beyond the ones discussed in this chapter. The use cases described in this chapter give you an excellent foundation for exploring other possibilities on your own.

Some of the common use cases of LXC and LXD come from the following requirements:

- The need for an isolated development environment without polluting your host machine

- Isolation within production servers and the possibility to run more than one service in its own container

- A need to test things with more than one version of the same software or different operating system environments

- Experimenting with different and new releases of GNU/Linux distributions without having to install them on a physical host machine

- Trying out a software or development stack that may or may not be used after some playing around

- Installing many types of software in your primary development machine or production server and maintaining them on a longer run

- Doing a dry run of any installation or maintenance task before actually executing it on production machines

- Better utilization and provisioning of server resources with multiple services running for different users or clients

- High-density virtual private server (VPS) hosting, where isolation without the cost of full virtualization is needed

- Easy access to host hardware from a container, compared to complicated access methods from virtual machines

- Multiple build environments with different customizations in place

© Senthil Kumaran S. 2017
S. Kumaran S., *Practical LXC and LXD*, DOI 10.1007/978-1-4842-3024-4_6

# Using the Pelican Static Site Generator

In this section we explore how to install and set up a static website using a static site generator called Pelican within a container. Pelican is written in Python.

Begin by creating an Ubuntu Zesty container called ubuntu-pelican with the following command:

```
$ sudo lxc-create -t ubuntu -n ubuntu-pelican -- --release zesty
```

Once the container is created, start and then log in to the container using the following commands:

```
$ sudo lxc-start -n ubuntu-pelican
$ sudo lxc-attach -n ubuntu-pelican
root@ubuntu-pelican:/#
```

As in any Debian-based system, it is always a good practice to make sure the system is up to date before installing any software on it. Updating the system ensures that you have the latest versions of software packages and that security updates (if any) are applied to the system. Do this with the following commands within the Ubuntu container we just created:

```
root@ubuntu-pelican:/# apt update
root@ubuntu-pelican:/# apt upgrade
```

Now that the system is confirmed to be up to date, we will install Pelican, the Emacs text editor, and net-tools, along with the Apache2 web server to serve static pages that will be generated by Pelican. The following command installs the necessary packages:

```
root@ubuntu-pelican:/# apt install pelican emacs25-nox net-tools apache2
```

Pelican is now installed in the container. We are ready to start a new website project with Pelican:

```
root@ubuntu-pelican:/# pelican-quickstart
Welcome to pelican-quickstart v3.7.1.

This script will help you create a new Pelican-based website.

Please answer the following questions so this script can generate the files
needed by Pelican.

> Where do you want to create your new web site? [.] demosite
> What will be the title of this web site? Demo Static Website
> Who will be the author of this web site? stylesen
> What will be the default language of this web site? [en]
> Do you want to specify a URL prefix? e.g., http://example.com   (Y/n) n
```

```
> Do you want to enable article pagination? (Y/n) y
> How many articles per page do you want? [10]
> What is your time zone? [Europe/Paris] Asia/Kolkata
> Do you want to generate a Fabfile/Makefile to automate generation and
  publishing? (Y/n) y
> Do you want an auto-reload & simpleHTTP script to assist with theme and
  site development? (Y/n) y
> Do you want to upload your website using FTP? (y/N) n
> Do you want to upload your website using SSH? (y/N) n
> Do you want to upload your website using Dropbox? (y/N) n
> Do you want to upload your website using S3? (y/N) n
> Do you want to upload your website using Rackspace Cloud Files? (y/N) n
> Do you want to upload your website using GitHub Pages? (y/N) n
Done. Your new project is available at /demosite
root@ubuntu-pelican:/#
```

With the preceding script, Pelican has bootstrapped our new website project in the directory /demosite:

```
root@ubuntu-pelican:/# cd demosite/
root@ubuntu-pelican:/demosite# ls
content          fabfile.py      output                  publishconf.py
develop_server.sh      Makefile      pelicanconf.py
root@ubuntu-pelican:/demosite#
```

During our Pelican quickstart, we have chosen to automate generation and publishing using a Makefile. Pelican has therefore created a Makefile in this directory, hence we also need make (a build tool) installed in the container to generate our static website:

```
root@ubuntu-pelican:/demosite# apt install make
```

As shown next, we create a pages directory inside the content directory to hold all the static pages of the demo site. Then, we create a home page in our demo site using the file home.md in content/pages/ directory, with the sample content.

```
root@ubuntu-pelican:/demosite# mkdir content/pagesroot@ubuntu-pelican:/
demosite# emacs content/pages/home.md
root@ubuntu-pelican:/demosite# cat content/pages/home.md
Title: My Home Page
Category: Home
Tags: pelican, publishing, demo, sample
Authors: Senthil Kumaran S

This is the home page of this demo site.
root@ubuntu-pelican:/demosite #
```

Now that we have our simple demo site with one page in it, let's generate the website using make as follows:

```
root@ubuntu-pelican:/demosite# make html
pelican /demosite/content -o /demosite/output -s /demosite/pelicanconf.py
Done: Processed 0 articles, 0 drafts, 1 page and 0 hidden pages in 0.08 seconds.
root@ubuntu-pelican:/demosite#
```

The preceding command generates the static files for the website within the directory output, as shown here:

```
root@ubuntu-pelican:/demosite# ls output/ -alh
total 36K
drwxr-xr-x 4 root root 4.0K Jun 10 17:12 .
drwxr-xr-x 4 root root 4.0K Jun 10 17:08 ..
-rw-r--r-- 1 root root 2.2K Jun 10 17:12 archives.html
-rw-r--r-- 1 root root 2.2K Jun 10 17:12 authors.html
-rw-r--r-- 1 root root 2.1K Jun 10 17:12 categories.html
-rw-r--r-- 1 root root 2.1K Jun 10 17:12 index.html
drwxr-xr-x 2 root root 4.0K Jun 10 17:12 pages
-rw-r--r-- 1 root root 2.2K Jun 10 17:12 tags.html
drwxr-xr-x 4 root root 4.0K Jun 10 17:08 theme
root@ubuntu-pelican:/demosite#
```

Next, we copy the website contents to the Apache2 web root directory from which our website will get served by the Apache2 web server:

```
root@ubuntu-pelican:/demosite# cp output/* /var/www/html/ -rf
```

To access our newly published website, we need to find out the IP address of the container, using the following command:

```
root@ubuntu-pelican:/demosite# ifconfig eth0
eth0: flags=4163<UP,BROADCAST,RUNNING,MULTICAST>  mtu 1500
        inet 192.168.122.150  netmask 255.255.255.0  broadcast 192.168.122.255
        inet6 fe80::216:3eff:fee2:98da  prefixlen 64  scopeid 0x20<link>
        ether 00:16:3e:e2:98:da  txqueuelen 1000  (Ethernet)
        RX packets 72250  bytes 105161334 (105.1 MB)
        RX errors 0  dropped 0  overruns 0  frame 0
        TX packets 28468  bytes 1931727 (1.9 MB)
        TX errors 0  dropped 0 overruns 0  carrier 0  collisions 0

root@ubuntu-pelican:/demosite#
```

We now know the IP address of the container is 192.168.122.150. Accessing the website using this IP address using a web browser opens our demo site's index page as shown in Figure 6-1.

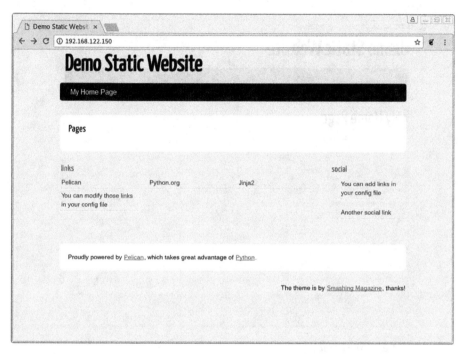

**Figure 6-1.** *Demo site generated by Pelican*

Clicking the *My Home Page* link on our demo site takes us to the home page shown in Figure 6-2.

**Figure 6-2.** *Demo site home page*

As demonstrated, we can publish a static website using the Pelican static site generator within an LXC container.

# Running Android CTS Within LXC

This is the main use case that caused me to start looking into LXC. To communicate with Android devices such as smartphones, tablets, and so forth, there are tools like fastboot and adb. The Android Compatibility Test Suite (CTS) is a suite of tests that is run on an Android device to check compatibility of the Device Under Test (DUT). CTS is a huge test suite that runs for a long time. It is driven by a host machine; the host will send tests to the DUT and collect test results as each test case completes on the DUT. Depending on the version of CTS you are running, there may be requirements for specific versions of Java and other tools installed in the host machine. This makes it difficult to maintain and use more than one version of CTS on the same machine. Using LXC in this scenario will help us to run CTS with an option of running CTS from different operating systems and different Java versions.

In this section, I will demonstrate running CTS from an LXC container running Debian Jessie. The DUT is a Nexus 4 phone with a factory image loaded and user debug mode enabled. The factory image of Android in Nexus 4 is Lollipop (i.e., 5.1.1, LMY48T). The CTS version is Android 5.1 R20 Compatibility Test Suite (CTS) - ARM, which was the latest compatible CTS available at the time of this writing. The setup is shown in Figure 6-3.

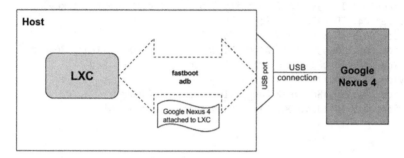

*Figure 6-3. LXC communication with Nexus 4*

---

■ **Note** This section assumes you have some Android knowledge, including how to work with Android tools such as fastboot and adb. Also, you should know how to get a DUT to fastboot and enable user debug mode.

Debian Jessie is our container operating system in this use case. Android 5.1 R20 Compatibility Test Suite (CTS) - ARM requires OpenJDK version 7.0, which is available in Debian Jessie. This is a great demonstration of the previously highlighted flexibility to run specific versions of software.

---

To start, create, start, and attach to a Debian Jessie LXC container:

```
$ sudo lxc-create -t debian -n jessie-cts -- --release jessie --packages
"systemd,systemd-sysv"
$ sudo lxc-start -n jessie-cts
$ sudo lxc-attach -n jessie-cts
root@jessie-cts:/#
```

As before, update and upgrade the packages within the jessie-cts container to make sure we have the latest packages and security updates:

```
root@jessie-cts:/# apt update
root@jessie-cts:/# apt upgrade
```

First, we will see how we can access an Android device from an LXC container via adb or fastboot. When the Nexus 4 is plugged in via the USB cable to my host machine, I see the following in the lsusb output:

```
$ lsusb
Bus 002 Device 005: ID 17ef:1013 Lenovo
Bus 002 Device 001: ID 1d6b:0003 Linux Foundation 3.0 root hub
Bus 001 Device 005: ID 138a:0017 Validity Sensors, Inc. Fingerprint Reader
Bus 001 Device 004: ID 5986:0706 Acer, Inc
Bus 001 Device 003: ID 8087:0a2b Intel Corp.
Bus 001 Device 002: ID 058f:9540 Alcor Micro Corp. AU9540 Smartcard Reader
Bus 001 Device 016: ID 0835:1601 Action Star Enterprise Co., Ltd
Bus 001 Device 015: ID 17ef:1013 Lenovo
Bus 001 Device 035: ID 18d1:4ee2 Google Inc. Nexus 4 (debug)
Bus 001 Device 001: ID 1d6b:0002 Linux Foundation 2.0 root hub
$
```

---

■ **Note**　lsusb is a command available via the package usbutils. Install usbutils with the following command, if it is not previously installed both in your host machine and within the LXC container jessie-cts:

```
$ sudo apt install usbutils
```

---

The preceding output shows the Nexus 4 (Google Inc.) is connected in USB bus 001 as device 023. The actual path of the Nexus 4 device translates to the following:

```
/dev/bus/usb/001/035
```

Within the LXC, although the Nexus 4 appears in lsusb output as follows, adb or fastboot does not have access to this device yet:

```
root@jessie-cts:/# lsusb
Bus 002 Device 005: ID 17ef:1013 Lenovo
Bus 002 Device 001: ID 1d6b:0003 Linux Foundation 3.0 root hub
Bus 001 Device 005: ID 138a:0017 Validity Sensors, Inc. Fingerprint Reader
Bus 001 Device 004: ID 5986:0706 Acer, Inc
Bus 001 Device 003: ID 8087:0a2b Intel Corp.
Bus 001 Device 002: ID 058f:9540 Alcor Micro Corp. AU9540 Smartcard Reader
Bus 001 Device 016: ID 0835:1601 Action Star Enterprise Co., Ltd
Bus 001 Device 015: ID 17ef:1013 Lenovo
Bus 001 Device 035: ID 18d1:4ee0 Google Inc.
Bus 001 Device 001: ID 1d6b:0002 Linux Foundation 2.0 root hub
root@jessie-cts:/#
```

Install fastboot, adb, and all other required packages inside the container and try accessing the device as shown next. The LXC container cannot see the Nexus 4.

```
root@jessie-cts:/# apt install openjdk-7-jdk aapt android-tools-adb android-
tools-fastboot wget unzip
----------OUTPUT TRUNCATED----------
root@jessie-cts:/# fastboot devices
root@jessie-cts:/# adb start-server
root@jessie-cts:/# adb devices
List of devices attached

root@jessie-cts:/#
```

To make this device accessible from within the container, use the following command on the host machine. The DUT is in fastboot mode at this point.

```
$ sudo lxc-device -n jessie-cts add /dev/bus/usb/001/035
```

Now we can access the Nexus 4 via fastboot or adb within the container as follows:

```
root@jessie-cts:/# fastboot devices
04f228d1d9c76f39     fastboot
root@jessie-cts:/#
```

Reboot the DUT to use the Android operating system installed on it:

```
root@jessie-cts:/# fastboot reboot
rebooting...

finished. total time: 3.017s
root@jessie-cts:/#
```

Every time the Nexus 4 is disconnected from a USB port and reconnected (which also includes a reboot or reboot-bootloader), the device number within the USB bus changes, though the bus number remains the same. For example, after every reboot or disconnect, the device path will increment like the following:

```
after reboot:  /dev/bus/usb/001/035
after reboot:  /dev/bus/usb/001/036
...
after reboot: /dev/bus/usb/001/0NN
```

This behavior makes it difficult to refer to the DUT consistently, since every time you must check the output of lsusb to identify the device number. To make things more deterministic and easier, I added the following udev rule in /etc/udev/rules. d/51-android.rules:

```
SUBSYSTEM=="usb", ATTR{idVendor}=="18d1", ATTR{idProduct}=="4ee2",
ATTRS{serial}=="04f228d1d9c76f39", MODE="0666", GROUP="plugdev",
SYMLINK+="android-nexus4"
```

___

■ **Note** ATTRS{serial} and SYMLINK+="android-nexus4" can help us to uniquely identify the Nexus 4 device consistently and create a symlink for it, without worrying about the USB device number on the bus.

___

After adding the previous rule, reload the udev rules so that the rule will take effect without a restart to the host machine:

```
$ sudo service udev stop
Warning: Stopping udev.service, but it can still be activated by:
 systemd-udevd-control.socket
 systemd-udevd-kernel.socket
$ sudo udevadm control --reload-rules
$ sudo service udev start
```

With the preceding configuration in place, we get a device as shown here:

```
$ ls -alh /dev/android-nexus4
lrwxrwxrwx 1 root root 15 Jun 11 01:15 /dev/android-nexus4 -> bus/usb/001/036
$
```

Now it should be easier to add the Android device to the container with the following command:

```
$ sudo lxc-device -n ubuntu-cts add /dev/android-nexus4
```

Within the container, we can access the Nexus 4 via adb as follows:

```
root@ubuntu-cts:/# adb kill-server
root@ubuntu-cts:/# adb start-server
* daemon not running. starting it now on port 5037 *
* daemon started successfully *
root@ubuntu-cts:/# adb devices
List of devices attached
04f228d1d9c76f39     device

root@ubuntu-cts:/#
```

---

■ **Note**    When accessing a device within an LXC container via adb, ensure the host is not running an adb daemon too, otherwise it will mask the visibility of the adb device within the container.

---

Let's download CTS and unzip the compressed file with the following commands:

```
root@jessie-cts:/# wget -c https://dl.google.com/dl/android/cts/android-
cts-5.1_r6-linux_x86-arm.zip
root@jessie-cts:/# unzip android-cts-5.1_r6-linux_x86-arm.zip
----------OUTPUT TRUNCATED----------
root@jessie-cts:/#
```

We start running the CTS test as follows:

```
root@jessie-cts:/# ./android-cts/tools/cts-tradefed run cts --plan Android
--disable-reboot
Android CTS 5.1_r6
Using commandline arguments as starting command: [run, cts, --plan, Android,
--disable-reboot]
06-11 02:25:41 I/DeviceManager: Detected new device 04f228d1d9c76f39
06-11 02:25:41 I/TestInvocation: Starting invocation for 'cts' on build
'5.1_r6' on device 04f228d1d9c76f39
06-11 02:25:41 I/04f228d1d9c76f39: Created result dir 2017.06.11_02.25.41
06-11 02:25:41 I/CtsTest: ABIs: [armeabi-v7a]
06-11 02:25:52 I/04f228d1d9c76f39: Collecting device info
06-11 02:25:53 I/CtsTest: Start test run of 84 packages, containing 65,097 tests
06-11 02:25:53 I/CtsTest: Installing prerequisites
06-11 02:25:06 I/04f228d1d9c76f39: ----------------------------------------
06-11 02:25:06 I/04f228d1d9c76f39: Test package armeabi-v7a android.
JobScheduler started
06-11 02:25:06 I/04f228d1d9c76f39: ----------------------------------------
06-11 02:25:40 I/04f228d1d9c76f39: android.jobscheduler.cts.TimingConstraint
sTest#testCancel PASS
06-11 02:25:45 I/04f228d1d9c76f39: android.jobscheduler.cts.TimingConstraint
sTest#testScheduleOnce PASS
06-11 02:25:00 I/04f228d1d9c76f39: android.jobscheduler.cts.TimingConstraint
sTest#testSchedulePeriodic PASS
----------OUTPUT TRUNCATED----------
root@jessie-cts:/#
```

The same principle is used in Linaro Automated Validation Architecture (LAVA), which automates running a wide range of testing, including CTS on Android DUTs. To see some sample jobs that are run in LAVA and how results are collected, check out https://validation.linaro.org/. To discover more about LAVA, helpful documentation is available at https://validation.linaro.org/static/docs/v2/.

# Running Unit Tests in LXC

LXC containers can be used to run unit tests of different projects. LXC provides the flexibility to run unit tests on different operating systems and distributions. When scripted properly, it can prove to be a powerful tool to automate unit test runs across platforms. In this section we will see how to run unit tests for a Scrapy project on a Debian Stretch container. Scrapy is a fast, high-level web crawling and web scraping framework that is used to crawl websites and extract structured data from web pages.

Create the container with all the packages that we will use preinstalled during container creation:

```
$ sudo lxc-create -t debian -n stretch-scrapy-unit-test -- --release stretch
--packages "python,git-all,python-pip,python-setuptools,python-dev,libssl-dev,
tox,build-essential"
```

Let's start the container and clone the Scrapy git repository after attaching to the container:

```
$ sudo lxc-start -n stretch-scrapy-unit-test
$ sudo lxc-attach -n stretch-scrapy-unit-test
root@stretch-scrapy-unit-test:/#  git clone https://github.com/scrapy/
scrapy.git scrapy.git
Cloning into 'scrapy.git'...
remote: Counting objects: 45066, done.
remote: Compressing objects: 100% (22/22), done.
remote: Total 45066 (delta 6), reused 12 (delta 5), pack-reused 45039
Receiving objects: 100% (45066/45066), 15.38 MiB | 1.93 MiB/s, done.
Resolving deltas: 100% (24435/24435), done.
root@stretch-scrapy-unit-test:/#
```

From the `scrapy.git` directory, run `tox`. This installs all the dependencies required for running the Scrapy project's unit tests and then runs the unit tests as shown here:

```
root@stretch-scrapy-unit-test:/scrapy.git# tox
py27 create: /scrapy.git/.tox/py27
py27 installdeps: -rrequirements.txt, botocore, Pillow != 3.0.0, leveldb,
-rtests/requirements.txt
py27 inst: /scrapy.git/.tox/dist/Scrapy-1.4.0.zip
py27 installed: asn1crypto==0.22.0,attrs==17.2.0,Automat==0.6.0,backports.
shutil-get-terminal-size==1.0.0,blessings==1.6,botocore==1.5.65,bpython==0.16,
brotlipy==0.7.0,certifi==2017.4.17,cffi==1.10.0,chardet==3.0.4,click==6.7,
constantly==15.1.0,coverage==4.4.1,cryptography==1.9,cssselect==1.0.1,
curtsies==0.2.11,decorator==4.0.11,docutils==0.13.1,enum34==1.1.6,
Flask==0.12.2,funcsigs==1.0.2,greenlet==0.4.12,hyperlink==17.1.1,
idna==2.5,incremental==17.5.0,ipaddress==1.0.18,ipython==5.4.1
----------OUTPUT TRUNCATED----------
```

```
identity==17.0.0,simplegeneric==0.8.1,six==1.10.0,testfixtures==5.1.1,
traitlets==4.3.2,Twisted==17.5.0,urllib3==1.21.1,urwid==1.3.1,w3lib==1.17.0,
wcwidth==0.1.7,Werkzeug==0.12.2,zope.interface==4.4.1
py27 runtests: PYTHONHASHSEED='2963483774'
py27 runtests: commands[0] | py.test --cov=scrapy --cov-report= scrapy tests
============================ test session starts ===========================
platform linux2 -- Python 2.7.13, pytest-2.9.2, py-1.4.34, pluggy-0.3.1
rootdir: /scrapy.git, inifile: pytest.ini
plugins: twisted-1.5, cov-2.2.1
collected 1688 items
----------OUTPUT TRUNCATED----------
tests/test_cmdline/__init__.py .....
tests/test_settings/__init__.py ................................
tests/test_spiderloader/__init__.py ............
tests/test_utils_misc/__init__.py ....

============ 1669 passed, 5 skipped, 14 xfailed in 345.75 seconds ============
_____ summary _____
  py27: commands succeeded
  congratulations :)
root@stretch-scrapy-unit-test:/scrapy.git#
```

With the preceding simple steps, we get the convenience of being able to run unit tests on different platforms without needing to worry about installing software in our host machine. You can apply similar logic to set up complex development environments that require many types of software to be installed.

# Running an Application Inside LXC

To quickly run an application inside an LXC container, we can use lxc-execute, which runs the specific command inside a container previously defined by lxc-create. It also accepts a configuration file in order to define parameters that were not available during the original container creation. The specified command is run within the container via an intermediate process called lxc-init. The lxc-init process will be started as the first process with PID 1 and the application that we want to run will be started as PID 2.

We will create a Debian Stretch–based container with Apache2 preinstalled:

```
$ sudo lxc-create -t debian -n stretch-apache2 -- --release stretch
--packages "apache2"
```

As per normal, this command has created the container but has not started it.

Instead of starting the container normally, let's just start Apache2 in this container:

```
$ sudo lxc-execute -n stretch-apache2 -- /etc/init.d/apache2 start &
[2] 4862
[1]  Done                    sudo lxc-execute -n stretch-apache2 -- /etc/
                             init.d/apache2 start
```

```
init.lxc.static: initutils.c: mount_fs: 36 failed to mount /proc : Device or
resource busy
Starting Apache httpd web server: apache2AH00557: apache2: apr_sockaddr_
info_get() failed for stretch-apache2
AH00558: apache2: Could not reliably determine the server's fully qualified
domain name, using 127.0.0.1. Set the 'ServerName' directive globally to
suppress this message
.

$
```

The preceding command runs just the apache2 process within the container. The container info is as follows:

```
$ sudo lxc-info -n stretch-apache2
Name:           stretch-apache2
State:          RUNNING
PID:            4877
CPU use:        0.16 seconds
BlkIO use:      8.00 KiB
Memory use:     9.84 MiB
KMem use:       3.35 MiB
Link:           veth43CQKX
TX bytes:       796 bytes
RX bytes:       4.03 KiB
Total bytes:    4.81 KiB
$
```

# Rolling Out Memcached Instances with LXC

Memcached is a distributed, general-purpose memory object caching system. In this section we will see a simple way to roll out container-based Memcached servers with a default configuration. Save the following content to a file named memcached-init.sh:

```
#!/bin/sh

LXC_NAME=$1

# create the container with some packages in place.
sudo lxc-create -q -t debian -n $LXC_NAME -- --release jessie --arch
amd64 --packages systemd,systemd-sysv,memcached,emacs24-nox,openssh-
server,inetutils-ping,wget,netcat

echo "Created $LXC_NAME container successfully"

# start the container.
sudo lxc-start -d -n $LXC_NAME
```

```
# copy some files.
sleep 10
sudo cp -v ./memcached.conf /var/lib/lxc/$LXC_NAME/rootfs/etc/
sudo lxc-attach -n $LXC_NAME -- service memcached restart
sudo cp -v ./resolv.conf /var/lib/lxc/$LXC_NAME/rootfs/etc/
```

This script will create and run an LXC container with Memcached installed. The file contents of memcached.conf and resolv.conf are as follows, specifying the Memcached configuration and name servers, respectively:

memcached.conf file contents:

```
# memcached default config file
# 2003 - Jay Bonci <jaybonci@debian.org>
# This configuration file is read by the start-memcached script provided as
# part of the Debian GNU/Linux distribution.

# Run memcached as a daemon. This command is implied, and is not needed for the
# daemon to run. See the README.Debian that comes with this package for more
# information.
-d

# Log memcached's output to /var/log/memcached
logfile /var/log/memcached.log

# Be verbose
# -v

# Be even more verbose (print client commands as well)
# -vv

# Start with a cap of 64 megs of memory. It's reasonable, and the daemon default
# Note that the daemon will grow to this size, but does not start out holding this much
# memory
-m 1000

# Default connection port is 11211
-p 11211

# Run the daemon as root. The start-memcached will default to running as root if no
# -u command is present in this config file
-u memcache

# Specify which IP address to listen on. The default is to listen on all IP addresses
# This parameter is one of the only security measures that memcached has, so make sure
# it's listening on a firewalled interface.
-l 0.0.0.0
```

```
# Limit the number of simultaneous incoming connections. The daemon default is 1024
# -c 1024

# Lock down all paged memory. Consult with the README and homepage before
you do this
# -k

# Return error when memory is exhausted (rather than removing items)
# -M

# Maximize core file limit
# -r
```

resolv.conf file contents:

```
nameserver 8.8.8.8
nameserver 8.8.4.4
nameserver 192.168.1.1
```

---

■ **Note**    All the preceding files should be in the same directory.

---

Invoking the memcached-init.sh script to create and run the memcached-1 LXC container is shown here:

```
$ chmod +x ./memcached-init.sh
$ ./memcached-init.sh memcached-1
Created memcached-1 container successfully
'./memcached.conf' -> '/var/lib/lxc/memcached-1/rootfs/etc/memcached.conf'
'./resolv.conf' -> '/var/lib/lxc/memcached-1/rootfs/etc/resolv.conf'
$
```

Now our memcached-1 server is ready to use, listening on port 11211:

```
$ sudo lxc-attach -n memcached-1
root@memcached-1:/# netstat -ant
Active Internet connections (servers and established)
Proto  Recv-Q  Send-Q  Local Address        Foreign Address      State
tcp    0       0       0.0.0.0:22           0.0.0.0:*            LISTEN
tcp    0       0       0.0.0.0:11211        0.0.0.0:*            LISTEN
tcp6   0       0       :::22                :::*                LISTEN
root@memcached-1:/#
```

Rolling a second Memcached server is as simple as the following:

```
$ ./memcached-init.sh memcached-2
Created memcached-2 container successfully
'./memcached.conf' -> '/var/lib/lxc/memcached-2/rootfs/etc/memcached.conf'
'./resolv.conf' -> '/var/lib/lxc/memcached-2/rootfs/etc/resolv.conf'
$ sudo lxc-attach -n memcached-2
root@memcached-2:/# netstat -ant
Active Internet connections (servers and established)
Proto Recv-Q Send-Q Local Address        Foreign Address        State
tcp    0      0      0.0.0.0:11211        0.0.0.0:*              LISTEN
tcp    0      0      0.0.0.0:22           0.0.0.0:*              LISTEN
tcp6   0      0      :::22                :::*                   LISTEN
root@memcached-2:/#
```

We can quickly set up any number of Memcached servers with the preceding script and files in place.

# Doing a Live Migration with LXD

LXD provides a feature to checkpoint and restore containers. *Checkpointing* is saving a particular state of the container to disk and *restoring* is bringing back the container to a particular state from the saved checkpoint. When a checkpoint saved on one host is restored on a different host, that is called *live migration*. We will use Checkpoint/Restore In Userspace (CRIU) to do the live migration of containers.

To start, install CRIU on the host machine as follows:

```
$ sudo apt install criu
```

We will launch an LXD Ubuntu 16.04 container to illustrate live migration:

```
$ sudo lxc launch ubuntu:16.04 container1
Creating container1
Starting container1
$
```

A snapshot of the preceding container can be taken as follows:

```
$ sudo lxc snapshot container1 checkpoint-1
```

This results in a stateless snapshot where the container's state is not saved to disk:

```
$ sudo lxc info container1 | grep checkpoint-1
  checkpoint-1 (taken at 2017/06/11 08:08 UTC) (stateless)
$
```

When the state of the container is saved, we can restore the container from the snapshot and the container need not boot from scratch. Instead, it can boot and start running services with the state that was saved in the snapshot. To save the current states of the container to disk, use the following command:

```
$ sudo lxc snapshot container1 checkpoint-2 --stateful
$ sudo lxc info container1 | grep checkpoint-2
 checkpoint-2 (taken at 2017/06/11 08:09 UTC) (stateful)
$
```

Similarly, we can stop and start the container and preserve the state as follows:

```
$ sudo lxc stop container1 --stateful
```

The preceding command writes the container state to disk. If you look in the LXD storage area, you can see how this is stored:

```
$ sudo ls /var/lib/lxd/containers/container1/state
cgroup.img        fs-23060.img     mountpoints-12.img  rule-9.img
core-132.img      fs-33.img        netdev-9.img        seccomp.img
core-1.img        fs-89.img        netlinksk.img       sigacts-132.img
core-23057.img    ids-132.img      netns-9.img         sigacts-1.img
core-23058.img    ids-1.img        packetsk.img        sigacts-23057.img
core-23059.img    ids-23057.img    pagemap-132.img     sigacts-23058.img
core-23060.img    ids-23058.img    pagemap-1.img       sigacts-23059.img
core-33.img       ids-23059.img    pagemap-23057.img   sigacts-23060.img
core-89.img       ids-23060.img    pagemap-23058.img   sigacts-33.img
dump.log          ids-33.img       pagemap-23059.img   sigacts-89.img
eventpoll.img     ids-89.img       pagemap-23060.img   signalfd.img
fdinfo-2.img      ifaddr-9.img     pagemap-33.img      stats-dump
fdinfo-3.img      inetsk.img       pagemap-89.img      timerfd.img
fdinfo-4.img      inotify.img      pages-1.img         tmpfs-dev-47.tar.gz.img
fdinfo-5.img      inventory.img    pages-2.img         tmpfs-dev-53.tar.gz.img
fdinfo-6.img      ip6tables-9.img  pages-3.img         tmpfs-dev-54.tar.gz.img
fdinfo-7.img      ipcns-var-10.img pages-4.img         tmpfs-dev-55.tar.gz.img
fdinfo-8.img      iptables-9.img   pages-5.img         tmpfs-dev-56.tar.gz.img
fdinfo-9.img      mm-132.img       pages-6.img         tty.img
fifo-data.img     mm-1.img         pages-7.img         tty.info
fifo.img          mm-23057.img     pages-8.img         tty-info.img
fs-132.img        mm-23058.img     pstree.img          unixsk.img
fs-1.img          mm-23059.img     reg-files.img       userns-13.img
fs-23057.img      mm-23060.img     remap-fpath.img     utsns-11.img
fs-23058.img      mm-33.img        route6-9.img
fs-23059.img      mm-89.img        route-9.img
$
```

Detailed information on container1 shows the snapshots that are available as follows and the status of container1 as Stopped:

```
$ sudo lxc info container1
Name: container1
Remote: unix:/var/lib/lxd/unix.socket
Architecture: x86_64
Created: 2017/06/04 23:55 UTC
Status: Stopped
Type: persistent
Profiles: default
Snapshots:
 checkpoint-1 (taken at 2017/06/11 08:08 UTC) (stateless)
 checkpoint-2 (taken at 2017/06/11 08:09 UTC) (stateful)
$
```

Let's start the container, restoring its state:

```
$ sudo lxc start container1
$ sudo lxc info container1
Name: container1
Remote: unix:/var/lib/lxd/unix.socket
Architecture: x86_64
Created: 2017/06/04 23:55 UTC
Status: Running
Type: persistent
Profiles: default
Pid: 22560
Ips:
 eth0:   inet     10.186.2.185                   veth56JKGX
 eth0:   inet6    fe80::216:3eff:fe97:8202       veth56JKGX
 lo:     inet     127.0.0.1
 lo:     inet6    ::1
Resources:
 Processes: 8
 CPU usage:
        CPU usage (in seconds): 0
 Memory usage:
        Memory (current): 120.53MB
        Memory (peak): 125.00MB
 Network usage:
        eth0:
        Bytes received: 2.42kB
        Bytes sent: 426B
        Packets received: 19
        Packets sent: 5
        lo:
        Bytes received: 0B
```

```
         Bytes sent: 0B
         Packets received: 0
         Packets sent: 0
Snapshots:
 checkpoint-1 (taken at 2017/06/11 08:08 UTC) (stateless)
 checkpoint-2 (taken at 2017/06/11 08:09 UTC) (stateful)
$
```

Let's now migrate our container (container1) to another host that is already
configured with LXD. (The IP address of this host is 192.168.1.8 on my local network.)
Install CRIU in this host machine before attempting live migration. Let's make this host
listen on the network as follows:

```
$ sudo lxc config set core.https_address [::]:8443
$ sudo lxc config set core.trust_password secret
```

With the preceding setup on the host machine that has container1, add the host as a
remote, as follows:

```
$ sudo lxc remote add stylesen 192.168.1.8
Certificate fingerprint: 313437663133343362643663353335396535562373930323306462
346533366265646465386263326537326535356539653531333435646433966638373235393134
ok (y/n)? y
Admin password for stylesen:
Client certificate stored at server:   stylesen
$
```

We can now see stylesen is listed as a remote LXD server:

```
$ sudo lxc remote list
+----------+--------------------------------------+--------------+--------+--------+
|   NAME   |                 URL                  |   PROTOCOL   | PUBLIC | STATIC |
+----------+--------------------------------------+--------------+--------+--------+
| images   | https://images.linuxcontainers.org   | simplestreams |  YES  |  NO    |
+----------+--------------------------------------+--------------+--------+--------+
| local (default) | unix://                       |     lxd       |  NO   |  YES   |
+----------+--------------------------------------+--------------+--------+--------+
| stylesen | https://192.168.1.8:8443             |     lxd       |  NO   |  NO    |
+----------+--------------------------------------+--------------+--------+--------+
| ubuntu   | https://cloud-images.ubuntu.com/releases | simplestreams | YES | YES  |
+----------+--------------------------------------+--------------+--------+--------+
| ubuntu-daily | https://cloud-images.ubuntu.com/daily | simplestreams | YES | YES  |
+----------+--------------------------------------+--------------+--------+--------+
$
```

Before live migration, let's see what containers are available in our remote server 'stylesen:'

```
$ sudo lxc list stylesen:
+------+-------+------+------+------+-----------+
| NAME | STATE | IPV4 | IPV6 | TYPE | SNAPSHOTS |
+------+-------+------+------+------+-----------+
$
```

Migrate container1 to the remote LXD server 'stylesen:' using the following command:

```
$ sudo lxc move container1 stylesen:
```

Now the container is live migrated to remote LXD server 'stylesen:', thus listing our 'local:' LXD server will not have container1:

```
$ sudo lxc list local: container1
+------+-------+------+------+------+-----------+
| NAME | STATE | IPV4 | IPV6 | TYPE | SNAPSHOTS |
+------+-------+------+------+------+-----------+
```

On the remote LXD server 'stylesen:', we can see container1 migrated and started running:

```
$ sudo lxc list stylesen:
+------------+---------+-----------+----------------+------------+-----------+
|NAME        |STATE    |    IPV4   |IPV6            |    TYPE    | SNAPSHOTS |
+------------+---------+-----------+----------------+------------+-----------+
|container1|RUNNING  |10.186.2.185|fd42:17c8:cc98:282b:|PERSISTENT|   2       |
                      (eth0)      216:3eff:fe97:8202
                                  (eth0)
+------------+---------+-----------+----------------+------------+-----------+
$
```

Figure 6-4 depicts the live migration scenario.

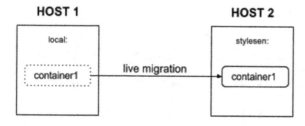

***Figure 6-4.*** *Live migration scenario*

Thus, LXD combined with CRIU provides a way to live migrate containers from one host to another, which may come in handy in many different scenarios.

# Running Other Architectures

LXC has a limitation of running based on the host's kernel architecture. Running armhf container on top of amd64 is not supported, since the underlying CPU does not know what to do with the new architecture that is requested. However, the ubuntu template can run other architectures by using the qemu-user-static package to invoke a specific architecture's emulator.

The qemu-user-static package provides emulators for different architectures. Some of the interesting architectures supported by qemu-user-static at the time of this writing are as follows:

- SPARC
- ARM
- AArch64
- PowerPC
- x86
- MIPS
- MicroBlaze

This opens up a huge range of possibilities to play around with different architectures without having actual hardware Consider, for example, building for a different architecture or setting up a build system that will build binaries on a different architecture. Install qemu-user-static as follows:

```
$ sudo apt install qemu-user-static
$
```

Once qemu-user-static is installed, we can have a look at the supported target emulator binaries that are available using the following command:

```
$ update-binfmts --display
qemu-aarch64 (enabled):
        package = qemu-user-static
        type = magic
        offset = 0
        magic = \x7f\x45\x4c\x46\x02\x01\x01\x00\x00\x00\x00\x00\x00\x00\x00\
x00\x00\x02\x00\xb7\x00
        mask = \xff\xff\xff\xff\xff\xff\xff\x00\xff\xff\xff\xff\xff\xff\xff\
xff\xfe\xff\xff\xff
interpreter = /usr/bin/qemu-aarch64-static
        detector =
qemu-microblaze (enabled):
        package = qemu-user-static
        type = magic
        offset = 0
```

```
    magic = \x7f\x45\x4c\x46\x01\x02\x01\x00\x00\x00\x00\x00\x00\x00\
    x00\x00\x00\x02\xba\xab
----------OUTPUT TRUNCATED----------
$
```

In the host machine, I can see the architectures enabled and their corresponding interpreter location as shown in Table 6-1.

***Table 6-1.*** *Emulator Architectures and Their Interpreter Location*

| Enabled Architecture | Interpreter Location |
|---|---|
| qemu-aarch64 | /usr/bin/qemu-aarch64-static |
| qemu-microblaze | /usr/bin/qemu-microblaze-static |
| qemu-arm | /usr/bin/qemu-arm-static |
| qemu-m68k | /usr/bin/qemu-m68k-static |
| qemu-ppc64le | /usr/bin/qemu-ppc64le-static |
| qemu-ppc64abi32 | /usr/bin/qemu-ppc64abi32-static |
| qemu-sparc64 | /usr/bin/qemu-sparc64-static |
| qemu-sparc | /usr/bin/qemu-sparc-static |
| qemu-mips64el | /usr/bin/qemu-mips64el-static |
| qemu-sparc32plus | /usr/bin/qemu-sparc32plus-static |
| qemu-ppc64 | /usr/bin/qemu-ppc64-static |
| qemu-ppc | /usr/bin/qemu-ppc-static |
| qemu-mipsel | /usr/bin/qemu-mipsel-static |
| qemu-alpha | /usr/bin/qemu-alpha-static |
| qemu-cris | /usr/bin/qemu-cris-static |
| qemu-mips | /usr/bin/qemu-mips-static |
| qemu-mips64 | /usr/bin/qemu-mips64-static |
| qemu-s390x | /usr/bin/qemu-s390x-static |
| qemu-armeb | /usr/bin/qemu-armeb-static |

# armhf Container

We will create an ARM-based container using qemu-user-static and ubuntu templates as follows:

```
$ sudo lxc-create -t ubuntu -n zesty-armhf -- --release zesty --arch armhf
--packages "wget"
Checking cache download in /var/cache/lxc/zesty/rootfs-armhf ...
Installing packages in template: apt-transport-https,ssh,vim,language-pack-en
```

119

```
Downloading ubuntu zesty minimal ...
I: Running command: debootstrap --arch armhf --foreign --verbose
--components=main,universe --include=apt-transport-https,ssh,vim,language-
pack-en zesty /var/cache/lxc/zesty/partial-armhf http://ports.ubuntu.com/
ubuntu-ports
I: Retrieving InRelease
I: Checking Release signature
I: Valid Release signature (key id 790BC7277767219C42C86F933B4FE6ACC0B21F32)
I: Retrieving Packages
----------OUTPUT TRUNCATED----------
update-initramfs: deferring update (trigger activated)
update-rc.d: warning: start and stop actions are no longer supported;
falling back to defaults
update-rc.d: warning: start and stop actions are no longer supported;
falling back to defaults
Setting up mountall:amd64 (2.54ubuntu1) ...
Processing triggers for libc-bin (2.24-9ubuntu2) ...
Processing triggers for dbus (1.10.10-1ubuntu2) ...
Processing triggers for systemd (232-21ubuntu3) ...
Processing triggers for initramfs-tools (0.125ubuntu9) ...
W: --force-yes is deprecated, use one of the options starting with --allow instead.

Current default time zone: 'Etc/UTC'
Local time is now:      Sun Jun 11 04:38:10 UTC 2017.
Universal Time is now:  Sun Jun 11 04:38:10 UTC 2017.

##
# The default user is 'ubuntu' with password 'ubuntu'!
# Use the 'sudo' command to run tasks as root in the container.
##

$
```

The host machine on which the container was created uses the amd64 (or x86_64) architecture, as shown here:

```
$ uname -a
Linux hanshu 4.10.0-21-generic #23-Ubuntu SMP Fri Apr 28 16:14:22 UTC 2017
x86_64 x86_64 x86_64 GNU/Linux
$ file /bin/pwd
/bin/pwd: ELF 64-bit LSB shared object, x86-64, version 1 (SYSV),
dynamically linked, interpreter /lib64/ld-linux-x86-64.so.2, for GNU/Linux
2.6.32, BuildID[sha1]=b8ff2ce5a5ef32ab15d8afb775a4c3e0ddd41e99, stripped
$
```

Now, let's start our newly created container based on armhf and verify the same as follows:

```
$ sudo lxc-start -n zesty-armhf
$ sudo lxc-attach -n zesty-armhf
root@zesty-armhf:/# uname -a
Linux zesty-armhf 4.10.0-21-generic #23-Ubuntu SMP Fri Apr 28 16:14:22 UTC
2017 armv7l armv7l armv7l GNU/Linux
root@zesty-armhf:/# file /bin/pwd
/bin/pwd: ELF 32-bit LSB executable, ARM, EABI5 version 1 (SYSV),
dynamically linked, interpreter /lib/ld-linux-armhf.so.3, for GNU/Linux
3.2.0, BuildID[sha1]=155a8b5547327c505dc2662b6bc8c86238a2e4bd, stripped
root@zesty-armhf:/#
```

Let's try installing the "hello" armhf Debian package and see if it works in this armhf container:

```
root@zesty-armhf:/# wget http://http.us.debian.org/debian/pool/main/h/hello/
hello_2.10-1%2bb1_armhf.deb
--2017-06-11 05:17:05--  http://http.us.debian.org/debian/pool/main/h/hello/
hello_2.10-1%2bb1_armhf.deb
Resolving http.us.debian.org (http.us.debian.org)... 64.50.236.52,
128.61.240.89, 208.80.154.15, ...
Connecting to http.us.debian.org (http.us.debian.org)|64.50.236.52|:80... connected.
HTTP request sent, awaiting response... 200 OK
Length: 54540 (53K)
Saving to: 'hello_2.10-1+b1_armhf.deb'

hello_2.10-1+b1_arm 100%[====================>]  53.26K   111KB/s    in 0.5s

2017-06-11 05:17:06 (111 KB/s) - 'hello_2.10-1+b1_armhf.deb' saved [54540/54540]

root@zesty-armhf:/# dpkg -i hello_2.10-1+b1_armhf.deb
Selecting previously unselected package hello.
(Reading database ... 14199 files and directories currently installed.)
Preparing to unpack hello_2.10-1+b1_armhf.deb ...
Unpacking hello (2.10-1+b1) ...
Setting up hello (2.10-1+b1) ...
root@zesty-armhf:/# which hello
/usr/bin/hello
root@zesty-armhf:/# /usr/bin/hello
Hello, world!
root@zesty-armhf:/#
```

# ppc64el Container

Similarly, let's try running the ppc64el architecture based Ubuntu Zesty container. ppc64el is a 64-bit Little Endian PowerPC architecture:

```
$ sudo lxc-create -t ubuntu -n zesty-ppc64el -- --release zesty --arch ppc64el
Checking cache download in /var/cache/lxc/zesty/rootfs-ppc64el ...
Installing packages in template: apt-transport-https,ssh,vim,language-pack-en
Downloading ubuntu zesty minimal ...
I: Running command: debootstrap --arch ppc64el --foreign --verbose
--components=main,universe --include=apt-transport-https,ssh,vim,language-
pack-en zesty /var/cache/lxc/zesty/partial-ppc64el http://ports.ubuntu.com/
ubuntu-ports
I: Retrieving InRelease
I: Checking Release signature
I: Valid Release signature (key id 790BC7277767219C42C86F933B4FE6ACC0B21F32)
I: Retrieving Packages
----------OUTPUT TRUNCATED----------
Current default time zone: 'Etc/UTC'
Local time is now:      Sun Jun 11 05:08:33 UTC 2017.
Universal Time is now:  Sun Jun 11 05:08:33 UTC 2017.


##
# The default user is 'ubuntu' with password 'ubuntu'!
# Use the 'sudo' command to run tasks as root in the container.
##

$
```

We will start the ppc64el architecture based container and see what is running inside it as follows:

```
$ sudo lxc-start -n zesty-ppc64el
$ sudo lxc-attach -n zesty-ppc64el
root@zesty-ppc64el:/# uname -a
Linux zesty-ppc64el 4.10.0-21-generic #23-Ubuntu SMP Fri Apr 28 16:14:22 UTC
2017 ppc64le ppc64le ppc64le GNU/Linux
root@zesty-ppc64el:/# file /bin/pwd
/bin/pwd: ELF 64-bit LSB shared object, 64-bit PowerPC or cisco 7500,
version 1 (SYSV), dynamically linked, interpreter /lib64/ld64.so.2, for GNU/
Linux 3.2.0, BuildID[sha1]=730338a76710095bd2b651ce823cc9c014333e0f, stripped
root@zesty-ppc64el:/#
```

Let's try installing the "hello" ppc64el Debian package and see if it works in this container:

```
root@zesty-ppc64el:/# wget http://http.us.debian.org/debian/pool/main/h/
hello/hello_2.9-2%2bdeb8u1_ppc64el.deb
--2017-06-11 05:23:04--  http://http.us.debian.org/debian/pool/main/h/hello/
hello_2.9-2%2bdeb8u1_ppc64el.deb
Resolving http.us.debian.org (http.us.debian.org)... 208.80.154.15,
64.50.236.52, 64.50.233.100, ...
Connecting to http.us.debian.org (http.us.debian.org)|208.80.154.15|:80...
connected.
HTTP request sent, awaiting response... 200 OK
Length: 50314 (49K) [application/octet-stream]
Saving to: 'hello_2.9-2+deb8u1_ppc64el.deb'

hello_2.9-2+deb8u1_ 100%[=================>]  49.13K   112KB/s       in 0.4s

2017-06-11 05:23:05 (112 KB/s) - 'hello_2.9-2+deb8u1_ppc64el.deb' saved [50314/50314]

root@zesty-ppc64el:/# dpkg -i hello_2.9-2+deb8u1_ppc64el.deb
Selecting previously unselected package hello.
(Reading database ... 14284 files and directories currently installed.)
Preparing to unpack hello_2.9-2+deb8u1_ppc64el.deb ...
Unpacking hello (2.9-2+deb8u1) ...
Setting up hello (2.9-2+deb8u1) ...
root@zesty-ppc64el:/# which hello
/usr/bin/hello
root@zesty-ppc64el:/# /usr/bin/hello
Hello, world!
root@zesty-ppc64el:/#
```

As demonstrated, we can run containers based on (almost!) any architecture with the help of the ubuntu template. Sometimes a suitable rootfs and some tweaks are required in order to make certain architecture work with the host machine's environment.

# Booting a VM Image in LXC

Running a raw-format image designed for a virtual machine in LXC is also possible. Obtain a raw disk image using wget as follows on the host machine:

```
$ wget http://images.validation.linaro.org/kvm/jessie.img.gz
--2017-06-11 15:06:38--  http://images.validation.linaro.org/kvm/jessie.img.gz
Resolving images.validation.linaro.org (images.validation.linaro.org)...
51.148.40.7
Connecting to images.validation.linaro.org (images.validation.linaro.org)
|51.148.40.7|:80... connected.
HTTP request sent, awaiting response... 200 OK
```

```
Length: 181109804 (173M) [application/x-gzip]
Saving to: 'jessie.img.gz'

jessie.img.gz          100%[==================>] 172.72M  1.23MB/s    in 2m 48s

2017-06-11 15:09:27 (1.03 MB/s) - 'jessie.img.gz' saved [181109804/181109804]

$
```

---

■ **Note**    In the `jessie.img.gz` image downloaded here, the first partition is its root partition.

---

Decompress the image as follows, which will create the file `jessie.img` in the current directory:

```
$ gzip -d jessie.img.gz
$ ls -alh jessie.img
-rw-rw-r-- 1 stylesen stylesen 954M May 29  2014 jessie.img
$
```

Use the following command to install kpartx, which is a tool used to create device maps from the available partitions in a raw image:

```
$ sudo apt install kpartx
```

Create necessary loop devices using kpartx as follows:

```
$ sudo kpartx -a jessie.img
$ ls /dev/mapper/ -alh
total 0
drwxr-xr-x  2 root root         80 Jun 11 15:13 .
drwxr-xr-x 21 root root 4.1K Jun 11 15:13 ..
crw-------  1 root root 10, 236 Jun 10 22:17 control
lrwxrwxrwx  1 root root          7 Jun 11 15:13 loop0p1 -> ../dm-0
$
```

Create an LXC configuration file named vm-img-lxc.conf with the following content:

```
$ cat vm-img-lxc.conf
lxc.network.type = veth
lxc.network.flags = up
lxc.network.link = lxcbr0
lxc.utsname = vm-img-lxc

lxc.tty = 2
lxc.pts = 2048
lxc.rootfs = /dev/mapper/loop0p1
```

```
lxc.arch = amd64
lxc.cap.drop = sys_module mac_admin
```

Now start the container and see how it boots the VM image:

```
$ sudo lxc-start -n vm-img-lxc -f vm-img-lxc.conf -F
Mount failed for selinuxfs on /sys/fs/selinux:  No such file or directory
INIT: version 2.88 booting
Using makefile-style concurrent boot in runlevel S.
findfs: unable to resolve 'UUID=e91502e4-0fcb-41f9-9147-8cec6d059660'
mount: block device pstore is write-protected, mounting read-only
mount: cannot mount block device pstore read-only
udev does not support containers, not started ... (warning).
Setting the system clock.
hwclock: Cannot access the Hardware Clock via any known method.
hwclock: Use the --debug option to see the details of our search for an access method.
Unable to set System Clock to: Sun Jun 11 09:48:46 UTC 2017 ... (warning).
findfs: unable to resolve 'UUID=e91502e4-0fcb-41f9-9147-8cec6d059660'
Activating swap...done.
Usage: mountpoint [-q] [-d] [-x] path
mount: you must specify the filesystem type
Cannot check root file system because it is not mounted read-only. ... failed!
mount: cannot remount block device UUID=e91502e4-0fcb-41f9-9147-8cec6d059660
read-write, is write-protected
findfs: unable to resolve 'UUID=e91502e4-0fcb-41f9-9147-8cec6d059660'
mount: cannot remount block device tmpfs read-write, is write-protected
mount: cannot remount block device tmpfs read-write, is write-protected
mount: cannot remount block device proc read-write, is write-protected
mount: cannot remount block device sysfs read-write, is write-protected
mount: cannot remount block device tmpfs read-write, is write-protected
mount: cannot remount block device devpts read-write, is write-protected
Activating lvm and md swap...done.
Checking file systems...fsck from util-linux 2.20.1
done.
Cleaning up temporary files... /tmp.
Mounting local filesystems...done.
Activating swapfile swap...done.
findfs: unable to resolve 'UUID=e91502e4-0fcb-41f9-9147-8cec6d059660'
Cleaning up temporary files....
Setting kernel variables ...sysctl: permission denied on key 'vm.min_free_kbytes'
failed.
Configuring network interfaces...Internet Systems Consortium DHCP Client 4.2.4
Copyright 2004-2012 Internet Systems Consortium.
All rights reserved.
For info, please visit https://www.isc.org/software/dhcp/
```

125

```
Listening on LPF/eth0/c6:f8:a6:45:f5:6c
Sending on   LPF/eth0/c6:f8:a6:45:f5:6c
Sending on   Socket/fallback
DHCPREQUEST on eth0 to 255.255.255.255 port 67
DHCPNAK from 10.0.3.1
DHCPDISCOVER on eth0 to 255.255.255.255 port 67 interval 3
DHCPREQUEST on eth0 to 255.255.255.255 port 67
DHCPOFFER from 10.0.3.1
DHCPACK from 10.0.3.1
bound to 10.0.3.24 -- renewal in 1597 seconds.
done.
Cleaning up temporary files....
INIT: Entering runlevel: 2
Using makefile-style concurrent boot in runlevel 2.
Starting enhanced syslogd: rsyslogd.
----------OUTPUT TRUNCATED----------
```

Use lxc-console as follows to log in to the container:

```
$ sudo lxc-console -n vm-img-lxc

Debian GNU/Linux jessie/sid debian tty1

debian login: root
Password:
Last login: Sun Jun 11 09:53:05 UTC 2017 on tty1
Linux debian 4.10.0-21-generic #23-Ubuntu SMP Fri Apr 28 16:14:22 UTC 2017 x86_64

The programs included with the Debian GNU/Linux system are free software;
the exact distribution terms for each program are described in the
individual files in /usr/share/doc/*/copyright.

Debian GNU/Linux comes with ABSOLUTELY NO WARRANTY, to the extent
permitted by applicable law.
root@debian:~#
```

Type <Ctrl+a q> to exit the console. The root password for the image is root.

Stop the container using the following command; there is no need to destroy since the rootfs is mounted via the loop devices.

```
$ sudo lxc-stop -k -n vm-img-lxc
```

# Using JuJu with LXD

JuJu is an application modeling tool that can be used to deploy, configure, scale, and operate software on both public and private clouds. JuJu supports LXD. In this section we will explore how to work with JuJu and LXD by installing everything in an LXD container except for JuJu and LXD itself on the host machine.

We install JuJu in our host machine with the following command:

```
$ sudo apt install juju
```

Let's start by creating a JuJu controller, which is the management service of JuJu. Install it as a separate LXD container as follows:

```
$ juju bootstrap localhost juju-controller
Since Juju 2 is being run for the first time, downloading latest cloud information.
Fetching latest public cloud list...
Updated your list of public clouds with 1 cloud and 11 cloud regions added:

        added cloud:
        - oracle
        added cloud region:
        - aws/ca-central-1
        - aws/eu-west-2
        - azure/canadacentral
        - azure/canadaeast
        - azure/uksouth
        - azure/ukwest
        - azure/westcentralus
        - azure/westus2
        - google/asia-northeast1
        - google/asia-southeast1
        - google/us-west1
ERROR creating LXD client: juju doesn't support ipv6. Please disable LXD's IPV6:

    $ lxc network set lxdbr0 ipv6.address none

and rebootstrap
$
```

As you can see, when JuJu is run for the first time, it updates its list of public clouds. The preceding command failed with an error indicating JuJu does not support IPv6, but helpfully provides the command that has to be run to disable IPv6 in LXD; hence, run the following command:

```
$ lxc network set lxdbr0 ipv6.address none
```

After disabling IPv6 in LXD, retry bootstrapping our JuJu controller:

```
$ juju bootstrap localhost juju-controller
Creating Juju controller "juju-controller" on localhost/localhost
Looking for packaged Juju agent version 2.0.2 for amd64
To configure your system to better support LXD containers, please see:
https://github.com/lxc/lxd/blob/master/doc/production-setup.md
Launching controller instance(s) on localhost/localhost...
```

```
- juju-d729dc-0 (arch=amd64)
Fetching Juju GUI 2.7.3
Waiting for address
Attempting to connect to 10.186.2.131:22                    .
Logging to /var/log/cloud-init-output.log on the bootstrap machine
Running apt-get update
Running apt-get upgrade
Installing curl, cpu-checker, bridge-utils, cloud-utils, tmux
Fetching Juju agent version 2.0.2 for amd64
Installing Juju machine agent
Starting Juju machine agent (service jujud-machine-0)
Bootstrap agent now started
Contacting Juju controller at 10.186.2.131 to verify accessibility...
Bootstrap complete, "juju-controller" controller now available.
Controller machines are in the "controller" model.
Initial model "default" added.
$
```

Confirm that the JuJu controller is running by using the following command:

```
$ lxc list juju
+--------------+---------+----------------------+------+----------+-----------+
|     NAME     |  STATE  |        IPV4          | IPV6 |  TYPE    | SNAPSHOTS |
+--------------+---------+----------------------+------+----------+-----------+
| juju-d729dc-0| RUNNING | 10.186.2.131 (eth0)  |      | PERSISTENT| 0        |
+--------------+---------+----------------------+------+----------+-----------+
$
```

To verify that JuJu is set up properly, use the juju status command as follows:

```
$ juju status
Model    Controller       Cloud/Region           Version
default  juju-controller  localhost/localhost    2.0.2

App  Version  Status  Scale  Charm  Store  Rev  OS  Notes

Unit  Workload  Agent  Machine  Public address  Ports  Message

Machine  State  DNS  Inst id  Series  AZ

$
```

The JuJu controller is set up successfully now. We can see that there is a JuJu GUI installed as part of the controller setup. We will take a look at the JuJu GUI in just a bit. Before accessing the GUI web application, get the credentials via the following command:

```
$ juju show-controller --show-password
juju-controller:
 details:
        uuid: 011cc077-c1b4-4323-847f-d78080093bfe
        api-endpoints: ['10.186.2.131:17070']
        ca-cert: |
        -----BEGIN CERTIFICATE-----
        MIIDrDCCApSgAwIBAgIUDSACo861iQXuFKZjFG+WoHzfyOcwDQYJKoZIhvcNAQEL
        BQAwbjENMAsGA1UEChMEanVqdTEuMCwGA1UEAwwlanVqdS1nZW5lcmF0ZWQgQOEg
        Zm9yIG1vZGVsICJqdWp1LWNhIjEtMCsGA1UEBRMkN2E3NzAzZmItZTY10SOoMjEz
        LThkYjAtMWE4NGNlMDgoN2E4MB4XDTE3MDYwNDEzMjcwMFoXDTI3MDYxMTEzMjcw
        MFowbjENMAsGA1UEChMEanVqdTEuMCwGA1UEAwwlanVqdS1nZW5lcmF0ZWQgQOEg
        Zm9yIG1vZGVsICJqdWp1LWNhIjEtMCsGA1UEBRMkN2E3NzAzZmItZTY10SOoMjEz
        LThkYjAtMWE4NGNlMDgoN2E4MIIBIjANBgkqhkiG9woBAQEFAAOCAQ8AMIIBCgKC
        AQEA5nhETDPrpixCklGf8SNyKUd1QQKOsDFumwz46HCWDxBOPXbJ58eVXAN7pM5Y
        1sKhrPIRXI+lQ/FWjlGFZVp1jBAG+Y+hNw+vk8Od+KAEimamv7uTFsSkBEGa7P8T
        k/7HFu+LpkrGcaP37NYFBNyq2iNap6OMrpJUv2WGF+/PvR3hE/sZIiE4+U9sDuGB
        k4Rj+IJPIzrL2gyKYobV9UmYPNhEaYrsUXv7mCRNaMIvxDabjFCpL8ycEjunSKN2
        vR+z5sZgcPyjqXqukRUOWH5BUxWNdXUJ3Rms4G4nvgZlOAjPlQa+ujAU1rh6/z1C
        UqAyaLMv5OFJDWOKOigFGdHROQIDAQABooIwQDAOBgNVHQ8BAf8EBAMCAqQwDwYD
        VROTAQH/BAUwAwEB/zAdBgNVHQ4EFgQUH3ZOs+HFIwvyTSulTBAflbykYi8wDQYJ
        KoZIhvcNAQELBQADggEBAMg/lfIQfpOSVW24zOOTgOQFpMUn2LOake+3qO5VwpF4
        5i3CERAAkOMgMVNOC7cZ4+RowNYUylrG+dCeDOTd+ZlvhlDZDhfdlE2G21tskd1R
        vmFG6CJg85IEKlQ29ZW9rITNyOJWVEZz/qDUIv9z49kS39A172xIH/ouujXISwK9
        SxBPHve3LNzoAh+PE25NgDywrhPXwjpWD9uL1XrD/g3heGE5zw7ckscXVutVS1OE
        LMWTXyck1Q/XSUH4SMHb4tj3y4ONEWySQjjKO2DAwklKC+Pjbwgkx6vvCvFz9L3i
        pBp6V8qOGtpuVHnOOUGVtHjQLtMPr87pl6YOe2ix/3w=
        -----END CERTIFICATE-----
        cloud: localhost
        region: localhost
        agent-version: 2.0.2
 controller-machines:
        "0":
        instance-id: juju-d729dc-0
 models:
        controller:
         uuid: dc86e29d-c9f4-4fb9-868e-db264fd729dc
         machine-count: 1
        default:
         uuid: 4a1c7ebd-aca2-4f83-89a2-07aace2fdcbf
 current-model: admin/default
 account:
        user: admin
        access: superuser
        password: 9b520684687f26eadda5bf3df94b37b5
$
```

The preceding output shows various information about the controller instance along with the account credentials for logging into the JuJu web GUI. Issue the following command to access the JuJu GUI in your web browser; if the command's attempt to open the GUI in a web browser fails, copy and paste the designated URL into a web browser:

```
$ juju gui
Opening the Juju GUI in your browser.
If it does not open, open this URL:
https://10.186.2.131:17070/gui/4a1c7ebd-aca2-4f83-89a2-07aace2fdcbf/
$
```

The web browser opens the login page, as shown in Figure 6-5, where you enter the credentials previously obtained via juju show-controller --show-password.

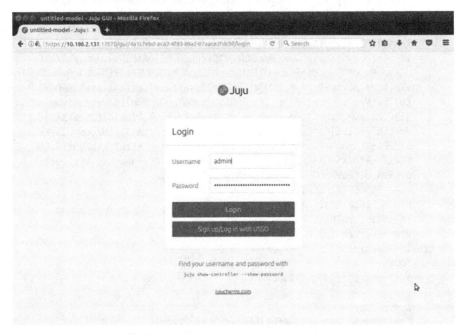

***Figure 6-5.*** *JuJu controller login page*

After entering the credentials and clicking *Login*, the JuJu controller GUI shown in Figure 6-6 is displayed.

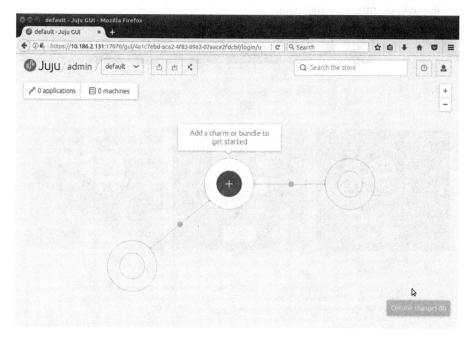

***Figure 6-6.*** *JuJu controller home page*

To deploy a charm or bundle using the JuJu controller GUI, click the green and white plus icon in the center of the screen showing the tooltip "Add a charm or bundle to get started," which should open the JuJu Store page as shown in Figure 6-7 (with helpful definitions of charms and bundles).

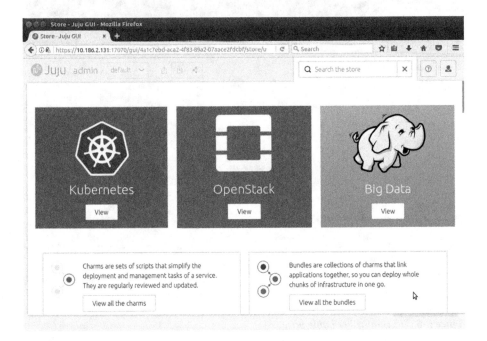

*Figure 6-7. JuJu Store*

Click the *View all the charms* button to view the recommended charms page. Scroll down the page and mouse over "rabbitmq server," which should show a green and white plus icon at the right side of the row, as shown in Figure 6-8. Click the icon to install the charm via JuJu.

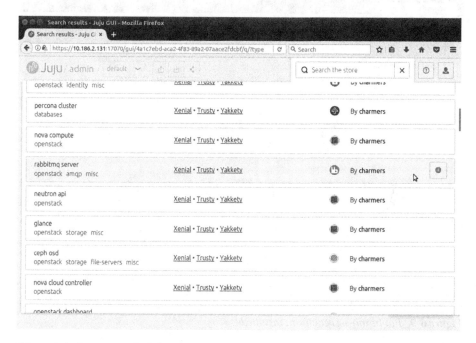

***Figure 6-8.*** *Recommended charms page*

Figure 6-9 shows the newly available charm, rabbitmq-server, on an LXD container on the JuJu controller GUI.

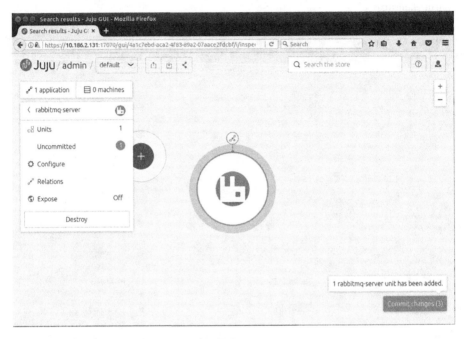

***Figure 6-9.*** *Rabbitmq-server charm installed*

As indicated in the button at the bottom-right corner, we need to commit the changes to deploy the actual LXD containers. Click the *Commit changes* button, which should open the Machines to be deployed page, as shown in Figure 6-10.

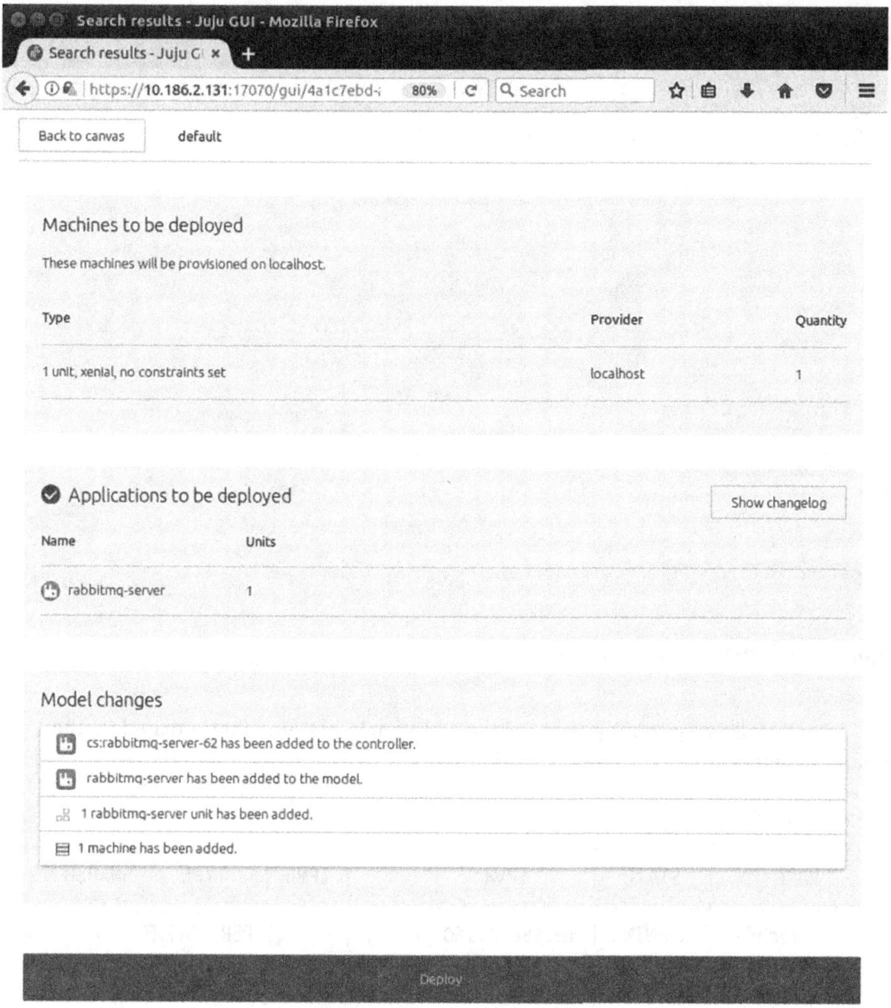

*Figure 6-10. Machines to be deployed page*

Click the *Deploy* button at the bottom of the page to deploy and start running the LXD container with rabbitmq-server installed. Figure 6-11 shows that rabbitmq-server is installed, with the rabbitmq-server icon in the JuJu controller GUI.

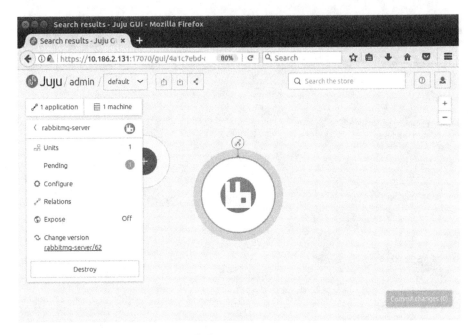

***Figure 6-11.*** *Rabbitmq-server installed in JuJu*

Use the following command to see the additional LXD containers created for the rabbitmq-server:

```
$ lxc list juju-
+---------------+---------+--------------------+------+------------+-----------+
|     NAME      |  STATE  |       IPV4         | IPV6 |   TYPE     | SNAPSHOTS |
+---------------+---------+--------------------+------+------------+-----------+
| juju-2fdcbf-1 | RUNNING | 10.186.2.160 (eth0)|      | PERSISTENT | 0         |
+---------------+---------+--------------------+------+------------+-----------+
| juju-d729dc-0 | RUNNING | 10.186.2.131 (eth0)|      | PERSISTENT | 0         |
+---------------+---------+--------------------+------+------------+-----------+
$
```

So far, we installed a "charm," a simple single server application in JuJu terms. Let's try installing a more complex application called a bundle in JuJu terms, which is a collection of services and can span across multiple LXD containers. Go to the JuJu Store page (as shown earlier in Figure 6-7) by clicking the green and white plus icon on the JuJu controller home page. On the JuJu Store page, click the *View all the bundles* button to open the recommended bundles page, as shown in Figure 6-12.

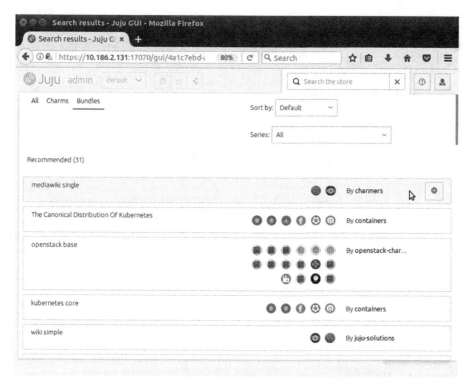

*Figure 6-12.* *Recommended bundles page*

Deploy the mediawiki bundle listed at the top of the recommended bundles in Figure 6-12 by hovering your mouse over it and clicking the plus icon. The mediawiki bundle requires a web server and a MySQL server, and is the simplest bundle spanning two LXD containers, as shown in Figure 6-13.

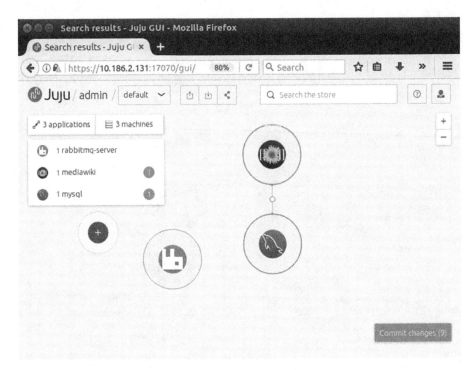

*Figure 6-13.* *Mediawiki JuJu bundle installed*

Click the *Commit changes* button to commit the bundle changes and deploy in order to start running the mediawiki bundle. View the additional containers created for running the mediawiki bundle with the following command:

```
$ lxc list juju-
+--------------+---------+----------------------+------+------------+---------+
|     NAME     |  STATE  |         IPV4         | IPV6 |    TYPE    |SNAPSHOTS|
+--------------+---------+----------------------+------+------------+---------+
| juju-2fdcbf-1| RUNNING | 10.186.2.160 (eth0)  |      | PERSISTENT | 0       |
+--------------+---------+----------------------+------+------------+---------+
| juju-2fdcbf-2| RUNNING | 10.186.2.225 (eth0)  |      | PERSISTENT | 0       |
+--------------+---------+----------------------+------+------------+---------+
| juju-2fdcbf-3| RUNNING | 10.186.2.87 (eth0)   |      | PERSISTENT | 0       |
+--------------+---------+----------------------+------+------------+----v---+
| juju-d729dc-0| RUNNING | 10.186.2.131 (eth0)  |      | PERSISTENT | 0       |
+--------------+---------+----------------------+------+------------+---------+
$
```

The LXD containers, such as juju-2fdcbf-2 and juju-2fdcbf-3, are created for the mediawiki bundle. Let's access the mediawiki bundle that was just deployed in an LXD container by accessing the IP address 10.186.2.225 in a web browser, where IP address 10.186.2.225 is the machine that will run the Apache web server in order to serve MediaWiki. Figure 6-14 shows MediaWiki running.

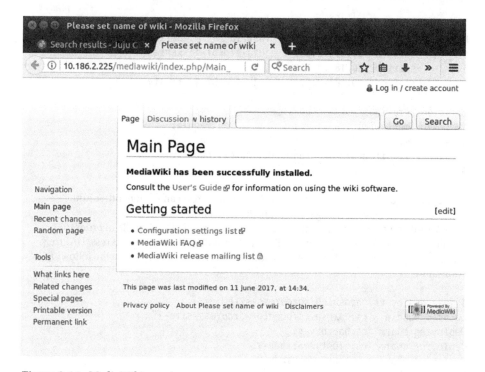

*Figure 6-14.* *MediaWiki running*

To find out which service each LXD container created by JuJu is running, use the following command:

```
$ juju status
Model    Controller      Cloud/Region        Version
default  juju-controller  localhost/localhost  2.0.2

App              Version Status Scale Charm        Store      Rev OS      Notes
mediawiki        1.19.14 active 1/1   mediawiki    jujucharms 3   ubuntu
mysql            5.5.55  active 1/1   mysql        jujucharms 29  ubuntu
rabbitmq-server  3.5.7   active 1     bitmq-server jujucharms 62  ubuntu
```

139

| Unit | Workload | Agent | Machine | Public address | Ports | Message |
|------|----------|-------|---------|----------------|-------|---------|
| mediawiki/1 | active | allocating | 1 | 10.186.2.225 | 80/tcp | Unit is ready |
| mysql/1 | active | allocating | 2 | 10.186.2.87 | 3306/tcp | Unit is ready |
| rabbitmq-server/0* | active | idle | 0 | 10.186.2.160 | 5672/tcp | Unit is ready |

| Machine | State | DNS | Inst id | Series | AZ |
|---------|-------|-----|---------|--------|----|
| 0 | started | 10.186.2.160 | juju-2fdcbf-1 | xenial | |
| 1 | started | 10.186.2.225 | juju-2fdcbf-2 | trusty | |
| 2 | started | 10.186.2.87 | juju-2fdcbf-3 | trusty | |

| Relation | Provides | Consumes | Type |
|----------|----------|----------|------|
| db | mediawiki | mysql | regular |
| cluster | mysql | mysql | peer |
| cluster | rabbitmq-server | rabbitmq-server | peer |
| $ | | | |

That is enough coverage of the JuJu GUI for now! You can explore other JuJu controller options by browsing through the JuJu GUI links.

We will now try bootstrapping a complex and scalable JuJu bundle in order to install WordPress from the command line. The bundle will install WordPress, HAProxy, Memcached, Nagios, and MariaDB on a total of six LXD containers. Run the following command:

```
$ juju deploy cs:~arosales/wordpress-site
Located bundle  "cs:~arosales/bundle/wordpress-site-3"
Deploying charm "cs:haproxy-41"
Deploying charm "cs:trusty/mariadb-7"
Deploying charm "cs:trusty/mariadb-7"
Deploying charm "cs:memcached-17"
Deploying charm "cs:nagios-15"
Deploying charm "cs:trusty/wordpress-5"
application wordpress exposed
Related "haproxy:reverseproxy" and "wordpress:website"
Related "wordpress:cache" and "memcached:cache"
Related "wordpress:db" and "mariadb:db"
Related "mariadb-slave:slave" and "mariadb:master"
Related "nagios:nagios" and "wordpress:juju-info"
Deploy of bundle completed.
$
```

It takes a few minutes for JuJu to create all the required LXD containers and start the services with the preceding wordpress bundle installation. Once it is done, issue the following command to see the six additional containers created:

```
$ lxc list juju-
+---------------+---------+---------------------+------+------------+---------+
|     NAME      |  STATE  |        IPV4         | IPV6 |    TYPE    |SNAPSHOTS|
+---------------+---------+---------------------+------+------------+---------+
| juju-2fdcbf-1 | RUNNING | 10.186.2.160 (eth0) |      | PERSISTENT | 0       |
+---------------+---------+---------------------+------+------------+---------+
| juju-2fdcbf-10| RUNNING | 10.186.2.83 (eth0)  |      | PERSISTENT | 0       |
+---------------+---------+---------------------+------+------------+---------+
| juju-2fdcbf-2 | RUNNING | 10.186.2.225 (eth0) |      | PERSISTENT | 0       |
+---------------+---------+---------------------+------+------------+---------+
| juju-2fdcbf-3 | RUNNING | 10.186.2.87 (eth0)  |      | PERSISTENT | 0       |
+---------------+---------+---------------------+------+------------+---------+
| juju-2fdcbf-5 | RUNNING | 10.186.2.142 (eth0) |      | PERSISTENT | 0       |
+---------------+---------+---------------------+------+------------+---------+
| juju-2fdcbf-6 | RUNNING | 10.186.2.21 (eth0)  |      | PERSISTENT | 0       |
+---------------+---------+---------------------+------+------------+---------+
| juju-2fdcbf-7 | RUNNING | 10.186.2.118 (eth0) |      | PERSISTENT | 0       |
+---------------+---------+---------------------+------+------------+---------+
| juju-2fdcbf-8 | RUNNING | 10.186.2.212 (eth0) |      | PERSISTENT | 0       |
+---------------+---------+---------------------+------+------------+---------+
| juju-2fdcbf-9 | RUNNING | 10.186.2.173 (eth0) |      | PERSISTENT | 0       |
+---------------+---------+---------------------+------+------------+---------+
| juju-d729dc-0 | RUNNING | 10.186.2.131 (eth0) |      | PERSISTENT | 0       |
+---------------+---------+---------------------+------+------------+---------+
$
```

With this installation in place, the JuJu GUI shows the wordpress bundle that was installed, as shown in Figure 6-15.

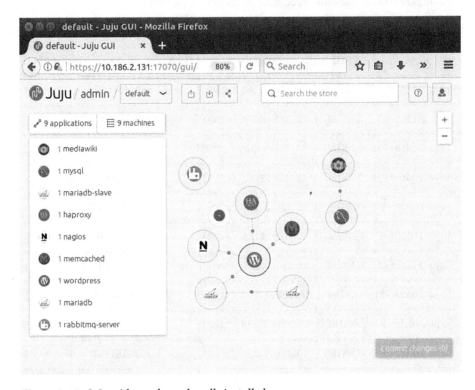

***Figure 6-15.*** *JuJu with wordpress bundle installed*

We can access the WordPress website via the `juju-2fdcbf-10` LXD container just created, whose IP address is 10.186.2.83. Upon accessing this container using a web browser, we see the installation page of WordPress ready, as shown in Figure 6-16.

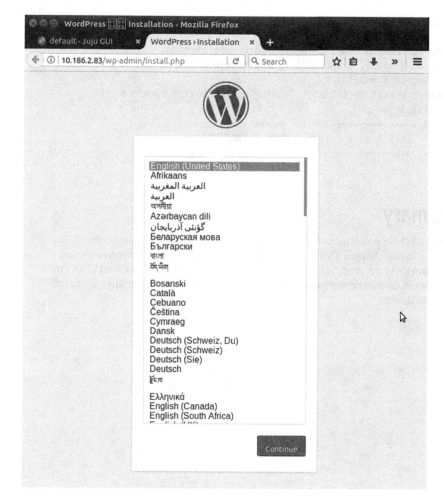

***Figure 6-16.*** *WordPress site running*

Other services installed as part of this bundle, such as haproxy, nagios, mariadb, and memcached, can be accessed on each of the LXD containers that got created using their respective IP addresses.

We can choose to destroy all the LXD containers created using JuJu at one shot by destroying the JuJu controller as follows:

```
$ juju destroy-controller juju-controller --destroy-all-models
WARNING! This command will destroy the "juju-controller" controller.
This includes all machines, applications, data and other resources.
```

```
Continue? (y/N):y
Destroying controller
Waiting for hosted model resources to be reclaimed
Waiting on 1 model, 9 machines, 9 applications
...Waiting on 1 model
All hosted models reclaimed, cleaning up controller machines
$ lxc list juju-
+------+-------+------+------+------+-----------+
| NAME | STATE | IPV4 | IPV6 | TYPE | SNAPSHOTS |
+------+-------+------+------+------+-----------+
$
```

# Summary

LXC and LXD are powerful container technologies that can solve many problems, as illustrated in this chapter. This is just an initial guide with some use cases to get you started, but there are many more use cases that could incorporate LXC and LXD. From development, to data center management, to deployment, the possibilities are vast with Linux containers.

# CHAPTER 7

■ ■ ■

# Containers and Security

Software is deemed to be production ready when it is secure. Security is highly important when dealing with operating systems, which is clearly what LXC provides using system-level containers. The basic idea of Linux containers is to share resources with isolated environments, and this raises a question about security. Is the isolation safe and is the resource sharing fair? When LXC started, many security considerations went unaddressed, but as LXC has evolved, many security features have been added, and the latest releases of LXC are considered secure based on certain recommended configurations, which we will explore in this chapter. LXD was designed from scratch to be secure, and it has also improved over time.

In LXC, security is ensured through the following:

- Control groups (cgroups)

- Capabilities

- AppArmor

- SELinux

- Seccomp

- User namespaces

Let's see how these features can be configured with LXC in order to make the LXC deployments secure. The configurations of these security features may differ depending on your use case.

## Cgroups

We discussed the resource allocation problem in Chapter 1, and how cgroups are used to control resource allocations to different processes. When using containers, we can set the cgroup values to control the resources allocated to each of the containers. Settings can either go into the LXC configuration file or be changed using the lxc-cgroup command. CPU and memory are very common resources that are controlled using cgroups, though cgroups can also be used for more complex resource constraints. The following lines in the LXC configuration file will set the CPU cores that this container can access, and restrict the memory for the specific container that is created with this configuration in place:

```
lxc.cgroup.cpuset.cpus = 0-1,3
lxc.cgroup.memory.limit_in_bytes = 1073741824
```

The first line says that the container can use the CPU cores 0, 1, and 3, (i.e., all except core 2 in a host that has four cores in total). The second line says that the maximum memory that the container can use is 1024MB (the limit is defined in bytes). The same values can be set using these `lxc-cgroup` commands:

```
$ sudo lxc-cgroup -n stretch-test cpuset.cpus 0,3
$ sudo lxc-cgroup -n stretch-test cpuset.cpus 0,3
$ sudo lxc-cgroup -n stretch-test memory.limit_in_bytes 1073741824
$ sudo lxc-cgroup -n stretch-test memory.limit_in_bytes 1073741824
$
```

These are just a couple of examples; there are more cgroups subsystems that could be controlled. See https://www.kernel.org/doc/Documentation/cgroup-v1/ to explore all the parameters that could be set using cgroups in LXC.

---

■ **Note** To use the `lxc-cgroup` command, the container should be in RUNNING state.

---

# Capabilities

The Linux capabilities support can be used to control the list of capabilities that should be retained or dropped when the container starts. The capabilities support was added to the Linux kernel from version 2.2; Linux divides the privileges available to "root" into distinct units. In the LXC configuration file, the following values are set in order to retain or drop capabilities:

```
lxc.cap.drop
lxc.cap.keep
```

For the complete list of available capabilities, have a look at the capabilities(7) manual page.

# AppArmor

AppArmor is a tool that allows administrators to restrict a program's capabilities with a per-program profile. To set an AppArmor profile, use the following parameter in the LXC configuration file:

```
lxc.aa_profile
```

Once this is set, the specified AppArmor profile will be applied before starting the container. Ubuntu 17.04 supplies the following standard AppArmor profiles with the default installation:

- lxc-default: This is the default profile that is loaded when lxc.aa_profile is unset.

- lxc-default-with-mounting: This profile allows mounting filesystems btrfs, zfs, etx4, and so on.

- lxc-default-cgns: This profile disallows mounting devpts, since there is a possibility to remount devpts if it is allowed.

- lxc-default-with-nesting: This profile allows container nesting, which is not restricted by default.

We can also write our own custom AppArmor profile and put it in the directory /etc/apparmor.d/lxc, from where it will be loaded by AppArmor when the new profile is defined in lxc.aa_profile and AppArmor is reloaded with the following command:

```
$ sudo service apparmor reload
```

# SELinux

SELinux is another kernel security facility, similar in scope to AppArmor. Different SELinux policies can be set using the following parameter in the LXC configuration file:

```
lxc.se_context
```

For this to work, it requires the operating system image that we are running in our LXC container to be built with SELinux support. In this case, LXC will enforce the SELinux policy just before starting the container. There is a default SELinux policy for RHEL, CentOS, and Oracle 6.5 in /usr/share/lxc/selinux/lxc.te, which can be chosen using the following in the LXC configuration file. The file itself has instructions for building the policy module.

```
lxc.se_context = system_u:system_r:lxc_t:s0:c62,c86,c150,c228
```

# Seccomp

Seccomp is a Linux kernel feature that was introduced in version 2.6.12. Seccomp restricts (filters) the system calls that a program may make. LXC can be configured to use a seccomp policy file, if one is available, via the following parameter in the configuration file:

```
lxc.seccomp
```

A simple seccomp policy file would look like the following, which allows just the syslog system call. Based on the use case for the container, different syscalls could be filtered for accesses from the container by the host's Linux kernel. Each of these syscalls should be referred to by ID instead of name. Unfortunately, the IDs differ from architecture to architecture.

```
1
Whitelist
103
```

To discover more details about seccomp, refer to its documentation.

# User Namespaces

LXC supports user namespaces, and this is the recommended way to secure LXC containers. User namespaces are configured by assigning user ID (UID) and group ID (GID) ranges for existing users, where an existing system user except root will be mapped to these UID/GID ranges for the users within the LXC container.

Based on user namespaces, LXC containers can be classified into two types:

- Privileged containers
- Unprivileged containers

## Privileged Containers

Privileged containers are started by the host's root user; once the container starts, the container's root user is mapped to the host's root user which has UID 0. This is the default when an LXC container is created in most of the distros, where there is no default security policy applied. This can give access to the host machine's resources when the root user from inside the container gains access to these resources. The only way to restrict that access is by using the methods previously described, such as seccomp, SELinux, and AppArmor. But writing a policy that applies the desired security that is required can be complicated.

When someone gains access to the host machine's root, that defeats the purpose of running isolated containers; an untrusted user can do harm to the host machine. If you trust the users of the containers, then using privileged containers is OK. But otherwise it is the most insecure configuration.

## Unprivileged Containers

Using unprivileged containers is the recommended way of creating and running containers for most configurations. In this case, the UID/GID ranges of users within the container are mapped to a less privileged account on the host system. Then, even if an attacker gains root access within the container, when the root gets mapped to the system user, there should not be any potential harm to the host machine—provided the system user to whom the user is mapped does not have sudo- or superuser-level privileges.

Unprivileged containers are implemented with the following three methods:

- `lxc-user-net`: A Ubuntu-specific script to create veth pair and bridge the same on the host machine.

- `newuidmap`: Used to set up a UID map

- `newgidmap`: Used to set up a GID map

To make unprivileged containers work, the host machine's Linux kernel should support user namespaces. User namespaces are supported well after Linux kernel version 3.12. Use the following command to check if the user namespace is enabled:

```
$ lxc-checkconfig | grep "User namespace"
User namespace: enabled
$
```

Let's look at how to set up unprivileged containers with UID/GID mapping. Add the following as part of the container configuration, which should enable the UID/GID mapping:

```
lxc.id_map = u 0 100000 65536 lxc.id_map = g 0 100000 65536
```

Then make the following changes in the /etc/subuid and /etc/subgid files to add the mapping to a specific user who will be running the container:

```
$ sudo cat /etc/subuid | grep "cole"
cole:100000:65536
$ sudo cat /etc/subgid | grep "cole"
cole:100000:65536
```

In this case, `cole` is a less privileged user on the host machine. With the preceding configuration in place, we could create unprivileged containers.

# Containers and Internet of Things (IoT)

The Internet of Things (IoT) is growing rapidly and there will be a huge number of connected "things" in the near future. This increasing number of devices that will be connected pushes every field of computer science to its limits and demands more. Security is of prime importance when so many devices are connected, and it is an active research topic in the IoT world.

We need innovative ways to deploy and manage the software installed on these IoT devices and to quickly update them with security fixes as they are released. Servers and other computers in use today tend to be bigger devices and there are smaller numbers of them compared to the scale at which these IoT devices are proliferating and will continue to grow in future. Managing these IoT devices to deliver software reliably is a major concern. Traditional software deployment, delivery, and updates are done via a pull model, where each of the computers pulls updates from a central server as and when they are available. If something goes wrong during these updates, there are well-established rollback methods, both automated and manual. These same methods do not scale in terms of IoT devices. Rather than asking users to keep their devices up to date, we need a mechanism that pushes updates in a reliable way to these devices. This mechanism should ensure the latest security updates reach these devices on time, and should not rely on the system administration skills of the users of these devices.

Containers can help in achieving a new mechanism to deploy and apply updates to these IoT devices, and many system-on-chip (SoC) vendors and other operating system vendors handling IoT devices are considering this mechanism. At a high level, the host operating system deployed on these devices will be a minimal operating system that is capable of running containers. The containers will run on top of these host operating systems in order to deliver various services that the IoT device is intended for. The host operating system should be hardened and, for the most part, should not be exposed to the outer world. It will act as a management commodity to manage containers installed on top of it.

The containers running on top of the host operating system can be either system-level or application-level containers, depending on the use case. There are certain advantages in establishing such an architecture for the IoT device software:

- Applying restrictions to the host operating system means fewer chances of breaking the devices.

- When updates are installed within containers, there could be a means to do a transaction-based update; when an update is misbehaving or erroneous, we can roll back the same within that container or simply replace the container.

- Updates can be applied reliably to the containers without disturbing the host operating system.

- Delivering updates can be done any number of times, as and when they are available, using a push mechanism to update different containers running within the device.

- Containers run in an isolated space, which will ensure that updates to one container will not affect the others when each of the containers is crafted with necessary isolation mechanisms.

Many IoT devices come with a dual boot partitions, which can be used to stage an update to the kernel before making it the default. When there is a new kernel update for the host operating system, it is applied to a secondary boot partition, which is then used to try booting the device. If it fails, the old boot partition is used. This can ensure that the device is not left in an inconsistent state after critical kernel updates. This is helpful to ensure the base or host operating system within the device is always working and can reliably push updates to containers running on top of it.

Devices also need to register to a cloud provider from which containers can get their updates. The updates are made available on the cloud and then devices registered to the cloud receive these updates and refresh their containers. Care should be taken to deliver these updates from the cloud to the device in a secure way by using methods like SSL, VPN, and so forth.

# Case Study: Ubuntu Snappy Core

Ubuntu Snappy Core is an operating system that works as described in the previous section to bring containerization to IoT devices. Ubuntu Snappy Core is developed by Canonical, the company behind the Ubuntu operating system. Ubuntu *snaps* are essentially fancy zip files that are secure, sandboxed, containerized applications isolated from the underlying system and from other applications. They are used to allow safe installation of apps on different devices and desktops.

The operating system snap is called the ubuntu-core. It is the first snap that will be installed, and it consists of a minimal rootfs to run and manage snaps. Subsequent snaps are installed on top of ubuntu-core.

Let's see a simple installation of a hello-world snap in our host machine, which runs Ubuntu 17.04. Before we start, ensure snapd is installed in the host machine. If not, install it with the following command:

```
$ sudo apt install snapd
```

snapd is a management system that helps in installing and updating snaps using a transactional mechanism and also manages the garbage collection of old versions of snaps. Similar to apt, use the snap command to install the hello-world snap from Canonical as follows:

```
$ sudo snap install hello-world
2017-06-15T06:51:29+05:30 INFO cannot auto connect core:core-support-plug
to core:core-support: (slot auto-connection), existing connection state
"core:core-support-plug core:core-support" in the way
2017-06-15T06:51:31+05:30 INFO cannot auto connect core:core-support-plug
to core:core-support: (slot auto-connection), existing connection state
"core:core-support-plug core:core-support" in the way
hello-world 6.3 from 'canonical' installed
$ cd /snap/hello-world/current
$ tree.
```

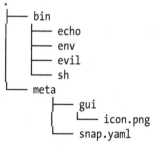

```
3 directories, 6 files
$
```

The important file here is meta/snap.yaml, which describes the snap with the security requirements and its integration with the system. The contents are as follows for the hello-world snap we just installed:

```
$ cat meta/snap.yaml
name: hello-world
version: 6.3
architectures: [ all ]
summary: The 'hello-world' of snaps
description: |
        This is a simple snap example that includes a few interesting binaries
        to demonstrate snaps and their confinement.
        * hello-world.env  - dump the env of commands run inside app sandbox
        * hello-world.evil - show how snappy sandboxes binaries
        * hello-world.sh   - enter interactive shell that runs in app sandbox
        * hello-world      - simply output text
apps:
env:
  command: bin/env
evil:
  command: bin/evil
sh:
  command: bin/sh
hello-world:
  command: bin/echo
$
```

To run the hello-world snap we just installed, use the following command:

```
$ which hello-world
/snap/bin/hello-world
$ hello-world
Hello World!
$
```

We can see all the snaps installed in this system using the following command:

```
$ snap list
Name          Version   Rev    Developer   Notes
core          16-2      1689   canonical   -
hello-world   6.3       27     canonical   -
$
```

There is also a GUI web application to manage snaps called Snapweb. It can be installed as follows as a snap itself:

```
$ sudo snap install snapweb
snapweb 0.26.1 from 'canonical' installed
$ sudo snapweb.generate-token
Snapweb Access Token:

SLzikVGA5aFeAF4JhE9mFj1uHepNOjaNgpHn7Y2yOTdnzPWChXp5ACKjIc7Mi4HW

Use the above token in the Snapweb interface to be granted access.
$
```

Snapweb runs on port 4201 and can be accessed via a web browser as shown in Figure 7-1. Use the token generated in the preceding output to log in to Snapweb.

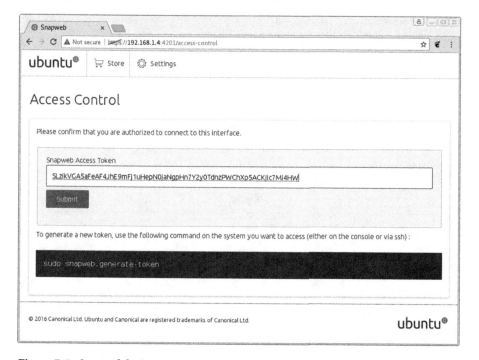

*Figure 7-1.* *Snapweb login page*

Once logged in, snaps can be managed using the simple Snapweb interface shown in Figure 7-2.

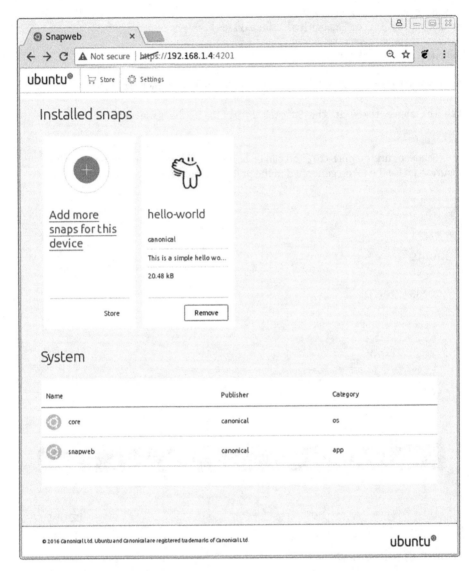

***Figure 7-2.** Snapweb dashboard*

The Snapweb interface is shown here only for demonstration purposes. It may not be practical on very small devices that are used for IoT, where instead the snap command-line tool is recommended.

# Summary

Containers can be secured by opting for unprivileged containers and using other security mechanisms available. Containers can also provide a mechanism to deploy, manage, and update software in IoT devices in a reliable way. We reviewed a case study of such an implementation with Ubuntu Snappy Core. There are other alternatives available using different containerization technologies and base operating system using more or less similar architectures to deliver software to IoT devices.

## Summary

# Index

## A, B

Android Compatibility Test
Suite (CTS), LXC
android device, add command, 106
configuration, 106
Debian Jessie, 103
DUT, 103, 106
install fastboot, 105
Nexus 4, 104–105
running, CTS test, 107
AppArmor, 146
Application inside, LXC container,
109–110
armhf container, 119–121

## C

Checkpoint/Restore In Userspace
(CRIU), 113
Container
application level, 2
control groups (Cgroups)
memory subsystem
hierarchy, 5–6
pseudo filesystem subsystem, 5
definition, 2
disk images, 8
history, 3
namespaces
Linux kernel, 7
network, 7–8
operating system level, 2
technology timeline, 4
traditional virtualization, 2
Control groups (Cgroups), 4–6

## D

Debian-based operating
systems, 18
Debian Stretch–based
container, 109
Debian template, 43–45
Default LXC templates
distribution-specific templates
Debian template, 43–45
Fedora template, 46–48
download template, 39, 41–43
Device Under Test (DUT), 102

## E

Emulator architectures, 119

## F, G, H

Fedora template, 46–48

## I

Images, LXD
copying, 54–55
deleting, 57
exporting, 58
formats
split image, 52–53
templates, 51–52
unified image, 49–51
identifiers, 53
importing, 55–56
viewing and editing
information, 56–57

© Senthil Kumaran S. 2017
S. Kumaran S., *Practical LXC and LXD*, DOI 10.1007/978-1-4842-3024-4

# Get the eBook for only $5!

Why limit yourself?

With most of our titles available in both PDF and ePUB format, you can access your content wherever and however you wish—on your PC, phone, tablet, or reader.

Since you've purchased this print book, we are happy to offer you the eBook for just $5.

To learn more, go to http://www.apress.com/companion or contact support@apress.com.

# Apress®

Printed in the United States
By Bookmasters